Marlene Coggins was a pretty child, with long fair hair, blue eyes, and a sunny nature.

The first sign of trouble was the discovery of Marlene leading a game of Doctors and Nurses behind a cupboard in the classroom. It was followed by Marlene being stuck on top of the climbing frame attracting a crowd of upward looking giggly boys. She had 'forgotten' her knickers.

Then there was the enchanting infant Jason, angelic looking, willing and winning who, when no one was looking, stuck his sharp pencil point into the arm of his small neighbour. The only child in the school not afraid of Jason was May Watts, fairly smelly, fairly dirty, fairly itchy, who was more than a match for the cherubic infant sadist.

There were children with rubbers stuck up their noses, children with impetigo, children who just wanted to be cuddled.

There were also the Forms from the Education Authority, and the men who didn't mend the leaky roof or the bulging walls or manage to stop electric sparks flying across the swimming pool.

St. Claude's was an enchanting, interesting, exciting – and fairly typical sc

Also by Elizabeth West

HOVEL IN THE HILLS
GARDEN IN THE HILLS
KITCHEN IN THE HILLS

and published by Corgi Books

SUFFER LITTLE CHILDREN

Elizabeth West

CORGI BOOKS

SUFFER LITTLE CHILDREN
A CORGI BOOK 0 552 12513 X

First publication in Great Britain

PRINTING HISTORY
Corgi edition published 1985

This book is set in 10/11 Times

Corgi Books are published by
Transworld Publishers Ltd.,
Century House, 61–63 Uxbridge Road,
Ealing, London W5 5SA.

Made and printed in Great Britain by
Hunt Barnard Printing Ltd., Aylesbury, Bucks.

. . .

Part of the Introduction has appeared in *The Staffroom Journal* – and my thanks are due to the Editor for his kind permission to reprint.

Contents

Introduction

The other day I was looking at a glossy catalogue we had just received from an organisation that sells primary school equipment. I was about to throw it into the wastepaper basket . . . (*do* Sales Managers realise that it is usually the school secretary who decides which catalogues end up on the staffroom table, and which in the wastebin?) . . . when my eye was caught by the photograph on the cover. It appeared to depict the advertiser's idea of what the average school office looks like. I stared in astonishment. A young lady with long hair, long legs and long fingernails, dressed in a classic suit from Aquascutum and with a pleasant and intelligent expression on her face was relaxing at a mahogany-veneered reproduction desk, and holding a telephone conversation with someone who was obviously pleasant and intelligent at the other end of the line. There was nothing much on her desk, other than a 'golf-ball' typewriter and a careful arrangement of documents. The room was carpeted throughout and the traditional academic touch was provided by a globe atlas and sports trophy on a side table, a tall glass-fronted cabinet of books, and a few tastefully-hung Constable prints on the wall.

Where had she put all the other things, I wondered? Where were the confiscated footballs, the abandoned badminton racquets, the lost property and the assortment of violins in battered cases ('Can we leave them in here Miss because there's no room in Class')? What had she done with the old cardboard boxes of tattered lampshades cracked tea sets and yellowing books left over from last term's jumble sale, and the piles of dated skirts, faded frocks and outsize trousers being collected for next week's 'As-Nu' stall? And where were all her *tins*? Every school secretary must have *tins* – old toffee tins, Elastoplast tins, or tobacco tins – for the dinner money, camp money, savings money, trip money, snack money, school fund, guitar-lesson money, etc. There is always another tin needed – so she collects them, and you can see them all around the room.

As for the advertiser's model – posing for the photograph in such expensive clothes – she wasn't very realistic either. (Someone should tell her what a school secretary earns; that would soon wipe the pleasant and intelligent expression from her face.) She was too young. All the school secretaries I know are middle-aged; they wear old jumpers and tweed skirts (in 'sensible' colours, not to show the dirt) and they sit behind cheap rickety wooden desks operating 30-year-old typewriters. The desk will have drawers that jam and handles that fall off when tugged. The typewriter will have several key tops held in place by Sellotape, and the ribbon-reverse mechanism won't work. The secretary will be bad-tempered. She will took up from her desk with an exasperated 'What *now*!' expression on her face. (An understandable attitude brought about by years of coping with the out-of-class needs of 5 – 11-year-old pupils.)

This is the only job I know of where you can return from lunch to find upon your desk one confiscated lead-weighted cosh, two confiscated obscene magazines, the remains of some peremptory First Aid treatment (such as a dirty and bloodstained swab of cotton wool and a demolished Elastoplast packet), a half-eaten apple, and a pair of wet knickers in a plastic bag with a note attached, 'Angela has done it again – have you a spare pair in the stock cupboard?'

Incidentally, all school secretaries soon learn that it is wise to go *out* to lunch if at all possible. I find that if I settle down quietly with my sandwiches and newspaper in the office I am interrupted by a constant stream of children asking:

Please Miss can I . . . have a football/skipping rope/
                              cricket bat
                              ring my mum
                              go down the shop for some crisps
                              come and sit with you
                              have a plaster for my knee
                              go home for my swimming things
or, worse still:
Please Miss . . . Susan's fallen off the climbing frame
                         Jason's just stuffed a toilet roll down the
                              bog
                         Ogunnaike's nose is bleeding
                         some big boys are beating up kids in the
                              infants' playground
                         Catherine's being sick in the corridor
It is slightly better if I go and hide behind the lockers in
the staffroom, where it is an accepted rule that the person
sitting nearest the door deals with the child knocking upon
it, but if that child is announcing . . . the phone is ringing
              a lady wants to see someone
              a man wants to . . . deliver clay/read the meters/
                              speak to the caretaker/mend the
                              broken window/use the phone
. . . then all members of staff will smile at me with that
helpless expression which means 'Well, of course, *you*
understand about these things don't you' – and, once
again, I put down my sandwiches and newspaper.

It is obvious that no such irritations ever cross the path of
that pleasant young lady on the cover of the catalogue.
How would *she* cope, I would like to know, with the
howling, gasping child that comes to her with a pencil
rubber stuck up its nose? And what would *she* say, I
wonder, to the member of staff who comes into the office
with a beaming smile, trailing a very sickly-looking infant,
and announcing, 'Rosemary's got a terrible cough (sore
throat / head lice / tonsillitis / chicken pox / scarlet fever /
impetigo) and shouldn't really be at school – so I thought
she had better *come and sit with you*.'

And yet I suppose that most people who have no daily
contact with the average state primary school might think
that the secretary's office does indeed look like the one in
the advertisement. Perhaps they think that a school

secretary occupies a dignified, scholarly position, where the only sounds to interrupt the calm of her days are the occasional tap tap of her typewriter and the distant soothing hum of children's voices chanting their tables, or lifted in song. But although such happy background sounds are quite often a pleasing accompaniment to my daily routine, it's not the whole story; there are other aspects to the life of a school secretary that very few people seem to know about. So, to present a more complete picture, I have compiled a record of the daily happenings at St. Claude's Primary School. It must be remembered, however, that the following chapters represent school life as seen from the school office – not the classroom – and my office at St. Claude's bears no resemblance whatsoever to the one illustrated on the cover of that glossy catalogue.

Staff List

Headteacher:	H. Masterton, B.A.
Deputy Head:	R. Appleby
Assistant teachers:	I. Singleton
	R. Scott, B.Sc.
	Miss H. Krantz
	Mrs E. Snow, B.Ed.

*　*　*

Ancillary Staff:	
School Secretary:	Mrs E. West
Cook/Kitchen Manageress:	Mrs M. Beagle
Kitchen Assistants:	Mrs E. Pin
	Mrs M. Sansom
School Meals Supervisory Assts:	Mrs E. Barron
	Mrs M. Binge
Caretaker:	H. Potts
Cleaners:	Mrs M. Potts
	Mrs J. Penfold

*　*　*

CHAPTER ONE

St. Claude's Junior Mixed & Infants' School

The School
Built in 1874, the school backs onto a steeply sloping grassy open space named, officially, St. Claude's Park but known locally as The Hill. In the 1920s (according to the Headmaster's log of the time) it was discovered that the school appeared to be sliding off the hill, and massive engineering works were undertaken whereby the school's foundations were 'chained' to the hillside, and the upper storey of the building was secured with stabilising bolts. In the 1960s, when the by-pass was built alongside the river, our neighbouring school of St. Cuthbert was demolished and the children were transferred to St. Claude's. In order to accommodate these extra children a two-storey wing was ad.led to the school. This flat-toppped pebble-dashed extension juts from the Municipal-Gothic gable end of the old school and has large windows. Occasionally footballs are kicked through these wide panes of glass and, for reasons of economy, three windows that were broken during the last year have stayed boarded up. The appearance of the rest of the school appears to have remained unchanged since Queen Victoria's reign. (The Victorian bell tower and the inner-city-Byzantine window arches are the subject of a Conservation Order. This was brought about mainly through the efforts of a few parents who are members of a local Amenity Preservation Group.)

The school has five classrooms, a library, gymnasium kitchen and dining hall; an Assembly Hall, art room pottery and small swimming pool. The swimming pool (built in the 1970s from funds raised by the PTA) hasn't been used for the last two years because of fears about the asbestos panels on the ceiling, and the badly corroded electrical heaters that send out large crackling sparks when the room is steam-filled. The pottery room isn't used much because of difficulties over plumbing. (Clay washed down sinks clogs up the system.) Asphalted playgrounds, surrounded by high stone walls, lie either side of the school. Stone-arched entrances (one bearing the word 'Juniors' and the other one 'Infants') lead into each playground. These Victorian directions are ignored. Children and parents use the entrance most convenient to them. The school's main front door (with corridor leading to the office) opens out onto a cobbled street.

Children and Parents

St. Claude's has around 160 children on its roll, and our catchment area extends down to the new double-carriage by-pass alongside the river, and also takes in all those streets surrounding The Hill. Once upon a time this open space stood as a natural boundary between the rich merchants in their Georgian mansions at the top of the hill, and the dock labourers in their hovels alongside the river at the bottom. To a certain extent this separation of the classes still applies, i.e. whereas some of the Georgian mansions are still in single-ownership (occupied by architects or television producers who spend a lot of money on sympathetic restoration work), the recently built block of Council flats occupies a sprawling site alongside the main road at the bottom of the hill.

But over the last few years changes have been taking place. The transient tenants of bed-sitterland have moved in amongst the Georgian mansions (and where this has happened the noble but crumbling houses have overflowing dustbins outside their gates equal to the number of tatty plastic bell-pushes beside the front door), and the Council flat tenants at the bottom of the hill have new neighbours too. Polytechnic lecturers and accountants are turning the dock labourers' hovels into bijou town cottages – carefully preserving the Victorian cast-iron doorknockers and putting tubs of geraniums outside the front windows. The conglomeration of classes continues. A speculative property developer – with an eye to the future when the disused dock area will become an inner-city marina – is building a complex of extremely expensive maisonettes within sight of the Council flats and within sound of the by-pass. But at the top of the hill another commune has taken over one of the mansions, and a Home for Battered Women has recently opened.

At the top of the hill there are leafy gardens and gracious tree-filled squares where unemployed men of indeterminate age, wearing bulky layers of dirty overcoat, sit clutching bottles and staring at the ground; all around the hill there are narrow alleyways linking streets that have broken glass in the road and motor bikes parked on the pavement; and at the bottom of the hill the traffic roars non-stop day and night along the by-pass. After dark no-one walks in any of these places.

From the houses, flats, bed-sitters and hostels of The Hill area come the children who attend St. Claude's School. The families are as diverse as the accommodation they occupy, but most of them can be very roughly divided into five distinct types:

Type 1. (Readers of *The Times* and *Telegraph*; probably vote Conservative)

Fathers are self-employed (either professionally or running small businesses) and we never see them at school. An au pair is sometimes employed, and the family runs two cars. Mothers (who usually drive their children to school) wear casual but expensive jeans, jumpers and jackets, and they take a conscientious interest in school affairs. They come in reliably, when asked, to take groups of children for cookery and needlework, or for recorder practice. They attend PTA meetings, but rarely have anything to say. These parents are usually married to each other and the relationships appear to be stable. Their children (who generally go home for lunch) are always clean and tidy. Little girls normally wear frocks – Viyella checks, Laura Ashley prints or charming Victorian pinafore dresses of 'The Mouse' label. The children are average performers academically and are well-behaved. Almost without fail they are taken away from us during the third-year juniors in order to attend a private preparatory school.

Type 2. (Readers of the *Guardian*; probably vote Liberal, SDP or The Ecology Party)

Fathers (and sometimes mothers as well) are usually in employment – either within the Education Service (university and polytechnic lecturers, or schoolteachers) or within the Health Service (GPs, specialist consultants or dentists). There is also a handful working for television or radio. Many Type 2 parents are active members of a Community Association, and some of the mothers have artistic sidelines (pottery, or jewellery-making, etc.). Both parents usually attend PTA meetings and are extremely vocal. Many of this group do not own a second car (on principle) and mothers who are not employed walk their children to school. They also ride around on bicycles (usually with baskets on the front and fluorescent protruding flags on the back). They wear old jeans or long dirndl skirts, cheese-cloth blouses and sandals. They belong to (and sport the badges of) the CND, Friends of the Earth, or The Soil Association. A certain amount of partner-swapping (sometimes long-term) takes place between these parents. Their children stay to school meals (which they often forget to pay for) or bring a packed lunch of wholemeal bread and cheese sandwiches, yoghurt, nuts and raisins. The children are encouraged by their parents to 'think for themselves' and to take full responsibility for their actions. This means that some of them come to school wearing old jumpers with holes in the elbows, trousers (or skirts) that fail to fasten, and old plimsolls without laces. They are often unwashed. Many of the parents have holiday cottages in Wales and Cornwall. Their children are cheerful, articulate and above-average in reading and artwork, and they mostly go to the local comprehensive school when they leave us for their secondary education.

Type 3. (Residents of communes, hostels and bed-sitters; choice of newspaper and probable politics not known)

A diverse assortment – but most of them are single parents; the exceptions being the families accommodated by the Local Authority in a Hostel for the Homeless. The single-parent mothers range from the middle-class 'I-have-rejected-my-parents'-background' category, to the

18

working-class 'He-made-me-do-it' sort. The children from these backgrounds are equally diverse. Some are extremely self-assured. They know all about rights-in-the-playground; they know how to get second helpings out of the school cook, and they are obviously well equipped, mentally and physically, to cope with a constantly changing domestic background. Others are frightened and bewildered. They creep into the school office, expecting to be shouted at; they cower at the playground edge, expecting to be bullied; and they cringe at the back of the classroom, expecting to be 'shown up'. All these children have free school meals, and they are all temporary pupils. They stay with us two days – three weeks – or a term or two. Never longer.

Type 4. (Readers of the *Mirror* and *Sun*; probably vote Labour)
Fathers are hard-working wage earners and we never see them at school. Mothers are either not employed, or are working on a very casual and part-time basis, and they take a great interest in their children's progress at school. They are quick to complain if they feel their child is being neglected in the classroom or bullied in the playground. They rarely attend PTA meetings and, if they do, they never speak. They are eager to offer their services, when asked, to lend a hand in supervising infants on a coach outing, or at the swimming pool, but it is noticeable that on these occasions they give most of their time and attention to their own offspring. Their children are always clean and tidily dressed and they have frequent new clothes from Marks and Spencers or C & A. Some of the children from this group stay to school dinners, but mostly they bring substantial packed lunches of white bread and ham (or corned beef) sandwiches plus a packet of crisps and several bars of chocolate. Generally speaking the parents within this group are married to each other and the home life is stable. When they leave us for secondary school the children usually attend the local comprehensive, although some parents are obviously uneasy. At the time of transfer they are eager to accept invitations to look around their child's new school, and they often seek reassurance from the Head of St. Claude's school.

Type 5. (Many can't read – and they probably don't vote.) There are social problems within this group. Fathers are usually long-term unemployed, physically or mentally disabled, or absent. Mothers are often simple-minded, harassed, unable to cope with day-to-day tasks, inarticulate and dirty. Both parents are extremely reluctant to visit the school. The children, all of whom stay to free school meals, are often unkempt, unhappy and aggressive. They are usually academically well below their class-mates, although some show flair for artwork. These children usually stay with us from the infant stage until they leave for the local comprehensive school unless, in the meantime, they have been recommended for Special Education. They are often the subject of frequent correspondence with, and attention from, the Educational Psychologist, their own Social Workers, and various welfare organisations.

In the classroom and playground all five types of children work and play together. Samantha (whose father lectures at the University School of Engineering) may share a lift home with Annette (whose mother runs a secretarial agency), but her best friend is Tracey (whose parents keep a sweet shop), and she sits next to Marcus (whose father has just gone to prison for mugging an elderly lady). Children who spend their holidays pony-trekking across America, sailing on the Norfolk Broads, or visiting archaeological sites in Greece, share the same dinner tables as those children whose horizons are always bounded by the by-pass and The Hill.

There are interesting similarities between parents Types 1 and 4 (both are conservative in outlook, conventionally moral in behaviour, stable in domestic arrangements, and physically clean) – also between Types 2, 3 and 5 (all are liberal in outlook, casual in sexual morals, haphazard in domestic arrangements, and sometimes physically dirty). In the annual school photograph it is impossible to tell which children are from the middle-class and which from the working-class households. From time to time head-lice and fleas attack children from all groups indiscriminately.

Although most of the St. Claude's families can be

pigeon-holed into these five types we also have a few individuals who cannot be classified; parents who, although falling within the financial or social category of a group, in no way conform to its general attitudes.

Teaching Staff:
1. Headteacher: Henry Masterton, B.A. (Sociology) (Open University)
   Aged 52. Married, with 1 daughter. Has been Head of St. Claude's for 7 years. At present attending part-time In-Service educational courses on: 'Management issues of Community Education' and 'Computer Studies in the Primary Curriculum'. A popular man with staff, parents and children.
2. Deputy Headteacher/Teacher of 3rd and 4th year juniors:
   Ronald Appleby
   Aged 38. Married, with 1 daughter and 3 sons. Has been Deputy Head of St. Claude's for 3 years. Known to the children as 'Happy Appy'. A cheerful and enthusiastic man whose practical skills are always available for benefit of school and staff.
3. Teacher of 2nd year juniors: Irvine Singleton
   Aged 63. Married with 1 son who lives in Australia. Has taught at St. Claude's for 27 years and is looking forward to retirement next year. Mr Singleton is in charge of music throughout the school and he was responsible for the formation of the St. Claude's Early Music Group. A man whose high standards and unwavering dedication commands respect from staff, parents and children.
4. Teacher and Top Infants/1st year juniors: Roger Scott, B.Sc.Hons (Economics – Social Administration)
   Aged 28. Single. Has taught at St. Claude's for 2 years. Is a firm believer in the integrated-day form of primary teaching. Has a highly original approach to orthographic interpretation, and arranges stimulating classroom displays. A pleasant young man – extremely popular with the children.
5. Teacher of 2nd year infants: Helen Krantz
   Aged 44. Single. Lives with her elderly mother. Has taught at St. Claude's for 9 years during which time she

has worked devotedly to improve and enlighten the children in her care. A loyal and forthright person whose concern for the school in general has earned the esteem of staff and parents.

6. Teacher of Reception Class: Eleanor Snow, B.Ed.Hons (Drama and Social Psychology)

   Aged 33. Married – no children. (Husband is the Local Education Authority's Senior Adviser for Arts.) A caring teacher with a most professional approach to her work. Her interest in the wider issues of education has resulted in her serving, in an advisory capacity, upon the Education Committee's Forum for Nursery Education, and she also runs an evening course on 'Structuring play in the infant school'. Mrs Snow occasionally writes well-informed articles – some of which have been published in *Child Education*. Regarded with great affection by the children in her class.

Ancillary Staff:

Caretaker: Herbert Potts

Mr Potts is pleasant, good-tempered, highly skilled in practical matters, unflappable, courteous and tactful. This makes him a very unusual caretaker. School caretakers are reputed to be surly, bad-tempered, Bolshie, arrogant and rude, but – bearing in mind that they are probably the most overworked and put-upon employees of the Education Service – such attitudes are perhaps understandable. Strangely enough the caretaker is the only *essential* member of a school staff. (If you think that statement is an exaggeration, just consider this: if a school caretaker goes on strike then the local authority will close the school. If a teacher goes on srike there will be certain difficulties if the other teachers' unions won't let them accept responsibility for the children – in which case the one class will have to be sent home – but apart from that, school life will continue as normal. If I go on strike it will inconvenience nobody except the Head. If the Head goes on strike no-one will notice.) Mr Potts has lived all his life in this part of the city (as a boy he attended the old St. Cuthbert's School) and he is extremely lucky in having a wife who, as well as sharing his childhood memories of the area, works at St. Claude's as one of the cleaners, and echoes Mr Potts' personal concern for the welfare of the school and its neighbourhood.

Cleaner No. 1: Miriam Potts

Mrs Potts is, perhaps, even more remarkable than her husband in that as well as coping placidly with the day-to-day dirt and disorder of St. Claude's in two shifts of duty, she sees to the staff coffee every morning and will often return in the afternoon if an extra pair of hands is needed to sort out jumble or to make and serve tea to visitors. She is the mother of 3 children – all of whom are well-behaved and doing very nicely at secondary school.

Cleaner No. 2: Joyce Penfold

Mrs Penfold has been with us only 6 months and is already threatening to leave. She says that if it wasn't for the bus fares into the town centre she would leave tomorrow and get a job at Marks and Spencers where they have easy-to-manage and up-to-date equipment for their cleaning staff. (At St. Claude's we possess two bulky and heavy industrial vacuum cleaners – neither of which works very well and sometimes not at all. More often than not our ladies have to do a lot of work with mops, buckets, hand brushes and dustpans.)

Cook/Kitchen Manageress: Mabel Beagle

Mrs Beagle is employed by The Authority to cook dinners at St. Claude's for up to 160 pupils plus staff. She also has to recruit and supervise 2 kitchen assistants and keep precise and accurate accounts of her expenditure. Mrs Beagle is an imaginative cook. Her fruit flans, chocolate and coconut sponges and apricot gateaux encourage queues of 'second-helpers'. Her steak and kidney puddings make everyone realise how hungry they are, and the aroma of her roast pork and stuffing throughout the school will, I know, mean extra members of staff claiming that they had inadvertently forgotten to put themselves down for lunch and asking if they could be squeezed in. Mrs Beagle loves children who come up to her with eager eyes and an empty plate and say 'Is there any more?' Mrs Beagle is not fond of vegetarians.

Kitchen Assistant No. 1: Edith Pin

Mrs Pin is very thin, very small, and has been working in the kitchen with Mrs Beagle for 10 years. She is quick in her movements. She seems nervous and always has a very worried expression on her face. She will reply when spoken to, but I have never known her to initiate a conversation.

Kitchen Assistant No. 2: Mary Sansom

Mrs Sansom is the mother of two children in the school and will, if Mrs Beagle is not watching, put extra helpings of food upon the plates of her children. She also gives particularly large helpings to the male members of staff – much to the irritation of Miss Krantz and Mrs Snow.

Playground Ladies (official title: School Meals Supervisory Assistants): Elsie Barron and Mavis Binge

I have put Mrs Barron and Mrs Binge together because they are usually *seen* together – deep in conversation as they patrol the edge of the infants' playground. (They are not supposed to work like this. They have full charge of the children during the lunch hour and one of them should be supervising the juniors and the other one the infants. But whereas the infants are nice and sweet, and play gentle games like 'The Farmer's in his Den', the juniors are nasty and rough and play games like 'Bulldog', so the playground ladies prefer to hover together at the edge of the infants' playground.) Mrs Barron and Mrs Binge have great responsibilities (if a child receives a fractured skull through falling off the climbing frame the first question asked is 'Where was the Supervisory Assistant?') yet they are given no authority. Children may spit at, swear at or kick the shins of playground ladies and their only recourse is to report the matter to a member of the teaching staff.

School Secretary

The school secretary stands in a sort of no-man's land between the teaching staff and the other ancillary staff. I sometimes think that the structure of the staff in a Primary School could be compared with the domestic set-up within a middle-class Victorian household. The teachers represent The Family (with the Headteacher as Father); the caretaker, cook, cleaners, kitchen and playground staff are the butler, cook, maids and other servants; and the school secretary is the governess. The governess is allowed to dine with The Family, but she is not *of* them . . . or, as the old Head put it to me when explaining that I was entitled to use the staffroom, 'At St. Claude's we have no class distinction. The school secretary is treated as though she were a member of staff.'

The relationship between teaching and ancillary staff is quite delicately, but indelibly, defined. This is demonstrated by the almost feudal benevolence at Christmas. The teaching staff do not exchange presents but they collect amongst themselves to give the caretaker a £5 note (or a few packets of tobacco) and his wife a potted plant. Mrs Beagle, the cook, receives a bottle of middle-quality sherry, whilst her kitchen staff, the other cleaner and the playground ladies each receive a half-pound box of Cadbury's milk chocolates. I am given a one-pound box of Black Magic.

CHAPTER TWO

Start of Term – with roof leaks and other Diversions

There is a tradition observed by all *primary schools*, (note the italics; I have no idea about the goings-on at secondary schools) that on the day before the start of the autumn term all staff come to school for a few hours in the morning to prepare for the weeks ahead. The teaching staff – who feel noble about this sacrifice of half a day's holiday – potter about their classrooms rearranging desks, putting up wall displays and fixing pretty covers to their class registers. The kitchen staff – who don't feel noble, and grumble about the waste of time and effort – wipe over tables that were wiped over at the end of last term, re-wash crockery and cutlery that was washed at the end of last term, and brew up for a cuppa, chat and smoke until they feel they have spent enough time at school and can go home. School secretaries – who don't get paid for holidays and are therefore justified in feeling noble – come in to sort out the accumulation of six weeks' mail, type out the new class lists and pin up the new Academic Year Planner upon which the most important events of the year (like school holidays) can be marked in advance.

Don't for a moment think that I am complaining about this tradition; I wouldn't have it any other way. I don't know about other school secretaries, but I, for one, need this time to collect my wits. After six weeks away from school I can't remember the combination to open the safe (for this reason I have pencilled it on the back of the telephone directory); I have to sit and think for ten minutes in order to recollect my last hiding-place for the stock cupboard key; and I always find myself facing a folder full of my own jotted notes that were obviously of great significance when we broke up last July, but which mean absolutely nothing to me now.

Moreover I know that the day ahead – the first day of the new academic year – will be so chaotic, with parents asking questions I can't answer, and children eager with enthusiastic information I haven't time to listen to, that if I don't sort out some of the paperwork in advance I will have to spend a lot of time talking my way out of a state of office inefficiency that causes letters to remain unanswered, official forms to be lost, and messages to be not passed on. What's more, I must admit to actually *liking* this half-a-day in school before the start of the year. We are, all of us, glad to be back. The frayed nerves of the end of last term are now soothed and restored; the snotty remarks and bickering are all forgotten. We beam at each other with sun-tanned faces – and the school is bright and sweet-smelling with polish.

I can remember that last year, on this day before the start of term I sat in my office just before I went home, and looked around me with pleasure. Everything was ready for tomorrow. My desk was in order, the bookshelves were tidy, and all appointments had been entered on the Planner. From the corridor I could hear the regular staccato 'klunk!' of Miss Krantz's staple gun as she put up large clean sheets of paper which would soon be filled with paintings reflecting 'What I did in the Holidays' . . . and from the classroom just down the corridor I could hear Mr Singleton at the piano picking out the notes of 'Glad that I live am I' – always his choice for the first hymn on the first Assembly. The entry in my diary for that day is long and reflective.

The next day remains in my memory as a sort of grey fudge. This was the day that May Watts started with us. I can see her now – standing in front of my desk clutching a grubby plastic Tesco carrier bag – staring at me through grimy glasses and with a coldsore on her top lip. Her mother, a massive woman with ripples of drab grey overcoat cascading from chin to knee, was sitting beside the radiator, surrounded by a clutch of grizzling younger children. There was another woman there – well-dressed and nervous – with a terrified-looking little girl clutching her hand; the office was tumultuous with noise as the juniors burst in with their holiday photographs that I *must see* – or with presents for Mr Masterton. This was also the day that Jason Spragg pinched the caretaker's keys and dropped them down a grating in the playground, and that one of Mrs Snow's little ones fell through a window and I had to dial 999 for an ambulance. I recall all this rather vaguely because none of it is recorded. I was so exhausted after the first day at school that the only thing I wrote in my diary for Tuesday, 2nd September, was 'God what a day!'

When the idea for this book first occurred to me I thought of publishing my last year's diary more or less as I had written it. After all, what better way of telling the story of St. Claude's than to take you, a day at a time, through the school year. As each term unfolded, punctuated by the traditional festivals – as calm days followed chaotic ones – as children joined us and children left us – so you would follow me through the weeks, and by the time you had reached the end of the book you would know all about us. Well, so you might, if I had written my diary properly. But you can see from my comments on the entries of 1st and 2nd September that whereas the diary may tell you something about me, you won't get to know much about life at St. Claude's. There is something else wrong with my diary too. Flicking through its pages I notice a rather tedious imbalance of information . . . I keep on rabbiting on about leaking roofs, collapsing walls, and complaining 'Still no action on the swimming pool!'

Take last 22nd November, for example. I happen to remember the date because this was the momentous occasion when our Junior Early Music Group, accompanied by Mr Singleton, went up to the Albert Hall to take part in the Schools' Prom. And what was my diary entry for the day? '22nd November. Heavy rain again. More roof leaks. We've now got one in the staff toilet. The skylight over the lavatory pan is releasing a steady stream of water. Mr Appleby thinks it's funny. Says it proves the point that women – being so badly designed – were obviously God's afterthought for Adam. Mr Potts also thinks it's funny – but at least he's provided some paper towels for the ladies. Miss Krantz has been taking her umbrella in with her.'

I think that my preoccupation with the discomforts of daily life is understandable, and is one that is possibly shared by the staffs of other dilapidated schools in the country. The crumbling fabric of St. Claude's is therefore worthy of some comment; but I mustn't harp on it. I hope to cover the subject in this second chapter – and then not to mention it again.

The swimming pool problem can be dealt with in a few sentences. We have a small, shallow pool in which the infants are (or rather, *were*) taught to swim. (This was installed about 10 years ago and paid for by funds raised by the PTA.) About the time of the Asbestos Scare it was discovered that not only was the ceiling formed of crumbling slabs of asbestos, but also that the electric air heaters were rusty, corroded and faulty. (Mr Potts says that sometimes when the steam was thick and condensation heavy he could see and hear electric sparks sizzling across the room.) The men contracted to renew the ceiling couldn't operate until the new heaters were installed, and by the time the last electrical contractor had visited the school and put in his tender, soaring inflation had put the price of the cheapest tender way above the amount of money allocated for the job by The Authority, who then decided that perhaps gas would be cheaper and we had to start all over again with visiting gas contractors. The pool has now been out of action for nearly two years and a very interesting blue-black fungus is sprouting from the cracks between the tiles in the changing room. I have a file about $1\frac{1}{2}''$ thick in my cabinet on the subject of The Swimming Pool, in which letters of excuse follow letters of complaint, and it is so long since 'Infants Swimming' appeared on the timetable that most people have forgotten the pool's existence. Mr Potts, however, finds the pool room a convenient place to store his winter supply of salt for the playground – and visiting maintenance men use it to store their tools and ladders overnight.

Our roof leaks, however, are of much concern to everyone, and I would guess that this is a problem St. Claude's shares with other Victorian schools – all of which were no doubt soundly built in the last century but, through subsequent neglect and abuse, have become the leaking, draughty shells they are today. Whilst the leak over the staff toilet was the most *personally* inconvenient one (we have only the one, unisex, cloakroom) and the leak just inside Mrs Snow's classroom was the most dangerous-looking (water running from a large damp patch on the ceiling was dribbling down the light flex and dripping off the end of the bulb) the most damaging leak which involved such a waste of public money was undoubtedly the one over Mr Scott's classroom and the library. These two rooms occupy the top floor of the new extension and the flat roof over them started to give trouble within a few years of the extension being built.

We complained to The Authority. We frequently complained to The Authority. Sometimes they took notice of our complaints and sent along contractors with names like 'The Speedy Roofers' or 'A1 Roof Repair Co.' who arrived in tatty, cement-encrusted open-backed trucks carrying ladders, ropes, rolls of roofing felt and buckets of tar. The attentions of these roofing contractors usually kept the rain out of the top floor of the new extension thereafter for the next two or three rainstorms – and then the trouble started all over again. Things came to a head when a particularly long drawn-out rainstorm over one weekend brought the library ceiling down and The Authority then decided that a major roof repair was necessary.

They sent along Europa Roofing Ltd, who came with two shiny new trucks and a lot of scaffolding. We had now entered the mandatory era of the Health and Safety Act of 1974 (more of this Act later) which apparently decreed that the little parapet surrounding our flat roof was 16 cm. too low to be healthy and safe and so railings had to be erected. Europa Roofing Ltd. was with us for almost a week. Having erected their scaffold tube railings they applied several coats of bitumen to the whole roof and liberally re-sanded it. They refused to look at any of our other leaks (not within their contract they said) but at least we felt that Mr Scott's room and the library would be dry from then on.

We were wrong. The next time we had heavy rain Mr Scott noticed with interest that water was steadily trickling down two walls of his classroom and flowing over his 'History of Shipping' displays which included two rather expensive prints borrowed from the City Museum. A quick check in the library revealed that two walls in there were similarly affected and the rest of the morning was spent dragging desks and bookshelves away from walls and salvaging the remains of sodden books and pictures. When the rain eased at lunchtime Mr Potts went up onto the roof to investigate. He found (along the two outside walls, immediately adjacent to the parapet) nine neatly cut round holes where Europa Ltd's scaffolding had pierced the roofing felt. He made a very good botch repair to these holes (with plastic bags and glazing tape) and I added another letter to the already bulging file on 'Roof leaks; complaints to the LEA'. All the other roof leaks (we have one just inside the entrance hall, two in the boys' toilet and one in the corridor outside the staffroom) receive occasional attention from Messrs Speedy Roofers or A1 Roof Repair Co., and their like and Mr Potts always keeps a supply of buckets and bowls ready for new emergencies.

The latest one occurred yesterday. In my office. I arrived to find a steady drip of water falling from the skylight and an apologetic Mr Potts who said that there were now so many roof leaks he had run out of buckets and could I make do with an old jumbo-sized polish tin. Unfortunately this tin had to be placed about 3' away from the door and children who came rushing in to see me kept kicking it over. After the third occasion when a large polish can full of rainwater was booted across the office I decided to remove it and put down some newspapers instead to sop up the leak. The office didn't get any wetter – and at least the wet didn't travel so far so violently.

The saga of the collapsing staffroom wall started last summer when, on a routine visit by a representative of The Authority's Maintenance Department, it was noticed that a wall overlooking the infants' playground was bulging. (We get these routine visits from The Authority's Maintenance Department from time to time. Their representative will wander around the school, making notes upon a clipboard, and promising us all sorts of exciting new things like extra toilet accommodation for the staff, renewal of rotting window frames, replacement of faulty locks and window latches and many other minor improvements – most of which never happen.) On this particular occasion last summer I was accompanying the Maintenance Department representative around the school when, on passing through the infant playground, he pointed at the towering wall of the staffroom. 'Look at that bulge,' he said. I looked. Sure enough the wall was slightly bulging. But as the wall was built of random stone rubble, and I had always thought the odd bulge or two could be accommodated by such building methods, I couldn't immediately see the reason for his alarm. 'I must report this to the Health and Safety Department,' he said.

I think that a few comments are called for here about the Health and Safety Act of 1974, and its effect upon schools. As I understand it, the purpose of the Act was to ensure, by means of legislation, that all people should work in a healthy and safe environment. The requirements of the Act are such that many establishments employing people in old premises will have to make major structural alterations in order to conform to the Act's provisions. For this reason a certain time lapse was allowed, during which the provisions of the Act were merely 'recommendations'; but these recommendations were to become mandatory within a prescribed time. The complicated ramifications of the Act are such that our Local Authority set up a Department to deal with it. At St. Claude's we first became aware of this department's existence when we began to receive letters from it. Long letters. Sometimes six-page letters (double-sided A4) with headings like 'Notification of Accidents and Dangerous Occurrences Regs. (Amended) 1980' and 'Minimum Provisions relating to Washing Facilities and Drying Clothes'.

Neither Mr Masterton nor I had time to actually *read* these letters, but when the fourth one arrived I realised that The Health and Safety Act of 1974 was something that couldn't be ignored, and so I opened a special file for it and sandwiched it between 'Health – Medical Inspections' and 'Junior Reading Test Results' in my filing cabinet. Then one day there came a letter which caught my attention because its heading of 'Health and Safety Representative – Primary Schools' suggested that this letter actually needed some action on our part. So I read it. I gathered that The Authority was asking each primary school to elect a member of staff who would hold himself/herself responsible for Health and Safety within the school premises, and that the name of the person so elected was to be notified to The Authority. I drew Mr Masterton's attention to this letter, and he raised the matter at the next staff meeting.

When he asked for a volunteer for the post there was a short, but very significant, silence as each member of staff chewed over the implications of this item on the agenda. First of all, what was The Authority really *up to*? Was local government being leaned on by national government and were they trying to pass the buck down to the poor fool on the spot who would bear the responsibility if something happened that could be construed as being neither healthy nor safe? On the other hand, would volunteering for such a post stand one in good stead when applying for senior posts at other schools, e.g. '. . . and for 4 years I was Health and Safety Officer at St. Claude's Primary School, being totally responsible for all matters relating to the implementation of this Act . . . etc. etc.' It took only a few seconds thought for Mr Appleby to offer his services. (I knew he would. He has also taken on responsibility for the Cycle Proficiency Course, After School Badminton, and the Lunch Hour Stamp Club.) And so I handed over my Health and Safety Act of 1974 file to him without delay, and since then I have passed to Mr Appleby all further correspondence that has arrived on the subject.

So far so good. But then the forms started arriving. First of all we had new and improved accident report forms, then we had some Safety Inspection Forms, asking us to report 'unsatisfactory conditions', and finally came the Hazard Report Forms. We had only a few weeks to get used to the idea of Reporting Hazards, when we received notification telling us to scrap the old Hazard Report Forms (which were white) and substitute them with the new improved ones (which were yellow).

Once or twice we tried using these Hazard Report Forms. We complained of the new fire doors that open the wrong way; the central heating trench excavated across the playground that wasn't filled in properly; a large area of loose tiles about to descend upon the public footpath – and each time we received a prompt acknowledgement on a card, but no action whatsoever. Mr Masterton became convinced that all letters of complaint from schools received by The Authority were immediately fed to the shredder, until the day when, in a flippant mood, I completed a Hazard Report Form to complain of the fact that Mrs Potts had not received her supply of rubber gloves which were essential to protect her hands from the harsh detergents used to clean floors. We had an emergency delivery of a box of gloves within three days.

One of the problems with the Health and Safety Department is, I think, that its staff keeps on changing. And the resulting confusion is reflected in my diary in the weeks that followed the visit of the Maintenance Department representative who was concerned about our bulging wall. When on 20th October a Miss Bennett from the Health and Safety Department visited us I assumed, naturally, that she had come about this wall. But she had never heard of it. 'I've only just joined the department,' she explained, 'and I am going round schools checking up on the safety of handrails on stairways.'

On 2nd November I was enthusiastically greeting another Health and Safety Department representative. A man this time. 'Ah, you've come about our bulging wall,' I said. He looked puzzled. 'No, I've come about the kiln.' 'But the lady who came about the handrails said she would remind you about the wall.' He looked even more puzzled. He didn't know anything about the bulging wall or the lady of the handrails, 'but I know you've got a kiln and I have to inspect it.' After he'd finished making notes in our pottery room I tried to persuade him to look at our bulging wall as well, but he said he couldn't because he was 'kilns' not 'structures', but he promised to pass on the message.

I was more cautious with the man who came on 7th December. 'Have you come to look at the handrails, the kiln, the fire door, the playground trench, or the roof?' He looked alarmed. 'I don't know anything about all that . . . this report here says you've got a bulging wall.' He was with us for about an hour, solemnly inspecting the wall from outside (in the playground) and inside (in the staffroom). His conclusions were that the County Surveyor would have to decide whether or not it was necessary to take the wall down and rebuild it but, in the meantime, that part of the playground should be barricaded off and put out-of-bounds to the children. Six weeks went by before we had a visit from yet another man of the Health and Safety Department. This man looked more important than the others; he was wearing a navy blue pin-striped suit and was carrying a briefcase. He looked quite capable of making wall-demolition-type decisions. 'We've kept that part of the infant playground empty since your colleague was here in December,' I said, 'will something be done about it soon?' He looked quite blank. 'I've come to inspect your First Aid Equipment,' he said.

I am going to digress a moment to enlarge upon this particular man's visit. He wasn't a friendly man and he went through my First Aid box with a superior, slightly disgusted, look on his face. I stood there feeling uncomfortable as he groped around in the muddle of cotton wool, safety pins, tweezers and loose plasters that somehow always accumulate in the bottom of the box, and I hastily fetched him a paper towel to wipe off the cream which squirted over his jacket cuff as he came across a tube of Savlon without a top. By the time he had finished I had a very tidy, but almost empty, First Aid box. He had thrown out all the plasters, the antiseptic cream and the bottle of T.C.P.

'You no longer use all this stuff,' he said, handing me a new First Aid Handbook. 'When a child injures itself the wound must be washed with plain water and then left exposed to the air to heal.' 'But what if it's dripping blood?' I wanted to know, 'Then you have to apply a lint dressing and a bandage.' I said nothing. I was thinking of the juniors with their grazed knuckles and bleeding knees – and wondering how long a bandage fixed by me would stay on; I was thinking of the infants with their tumbles and bruises – and the floods of tears that are immediately quenched at the application of 'magic cream'. This man might know all about first aid – but he obviously didn't know about children. 'Moreover,' he went on, 'no attempt must be made to remove splinters from the skin, nor objects from the eye.' 'So what do we do?' I asked. 'You send for the parents and the child must have the object removed at the clinic or hospital.' I protested at this. 'What if the parents are out to work; and what if it's only a tiny little splinter anyway?' But I could see the man wasn't interested. He just shrugged his shoulders and started packing away his first aid leaflets into his briefcase.

Now I am the world's most bumbling first-aider. I do my best to comfort and patch up, but I know that I am rather *clumsily* sympathetic, and I am prepared to take advice from anyone – but, so far, this man was just making life more difficult for me. However, there was one aspect upon which I certainly felt the need of someone else's opinion, so I asked him for his: 'Would you tell me what the correct procedure is for a bleeding nose? I am never sure whether to sit the child at the sink with the head bent forward or just let the nose drip, or whether to sit it in a chair with a pad of wet cotton wool on its nose, with the head held back.' The man stopped. He undid his briefcase again and got out his first aid leaflets and flicked through them. 'It doesn't say,' he said.

After he had gone I sat for a while and reflected upon all that he had told me. I then fished the plasters, cream and T.C.P. out of the wastepaper basket and put them back into the First Aid box.

Returning now to our bulging wall . . . The weeks went by; winter passed into spring; the children got used to avoiding that part of the playground – and we all forgot about it until the day that Lavinia Broughall's mother (groping behind the cooker in the staffroom in order to retrieve someone's pancake that had landed there after a rather too energetic toss) discovered The Crack. Lavinia Broughall's mother takes a cookery class in the staffroom every Tuesday afternoon. She had never before had occasion to grope behind the cooker (*nobody* gropes behind the cooker; Mrs Potts sweeps *around* it most carefully) so we didn't know how long the crack had been there. But it was sufficiently wide, and sufficiently new-looking to alarm Mrs Broughall. She came to the office (still holding the fluff and dirt-encrusted pancake) and asked me to go and have a look. The $\frac{1}{2}''$ wide crack arose from the floorboards, disappeared at the window ledge, and then reappeared above the curtains as a fine line and travelled straight up into the ceiling.

Although it appeared to be only a crack in the plaster I thought I had better notify the Health and Safety

Department. The Health and Safety department weren't very interested because, they said, the matter had been passed to the County Surveyor's Department. I eventually found someone in the County Surveyor's Department who knew something about the bulging wall at St. Claude's, but he said the whole matter was in abeyance pending the decisions taken at the next County Finance Committee Meeting. I found great difficulty in persuading anyone to take a message to the effect that hitherto unnoticed cracks had appeared in the staffroom wall, but was eventually put through to a helpful girl who said she would make sure that the appropriate person knew about it. She did. At the end of the week a man from the Surveyor's Department came to inspect the crack. What's more, he came prepared to *do* something. At three places across the crack he cemented in little glass tubes called 'tell-tales' which, he said, would indicate whether or not there was further movement in the wall. 'If these tubes crack,' he said, 'we shall know definitely that the wall is shifting.' Half an hour after he had left, I inspected the glass tubes. They were O.K. First thing next morning I looked at them again. They were still intact – and so I forgot about them.

One morning three weeks later, when Mr Potts was giving me his daily list of Things to be reported to The Authority, he ended up his list of roof leaks, disintegrating guttering and loose tiles, with the comment, 'Oh, and those glass things in the staffroom have all snapped in half.' In a panic I telephoned the County Surveyor's Department, but discovered that the helpful girl I had previously spoken to had now been transferred to the County Home Help Service and nobody had yet been appointed to replace her. I was eventually allowed to speak to the Departmental Head who told me that he was sure we had nothing to worry about and that he would send someone along. The someone came yesterday. He chiselled out the broken tell-tales, and he cemented in some bigger stronger ones . . . and there the matter rests.

I have now brought you up to date with the current position regarding the swimming pool, the roof leaks and the bulging wall at St. Claude's. At the end of each long summer holiday I return to school hoping that some, if not all, of these matters will have been attended to, but things are always just as we left them in July. (There seems to be some sort of Murphy's Law which decrees that *other* schools get the visiting contractors during school holidays, and any allocated to us arrive during the first week of term when maximum disruption to school life can be assured.)

But in spite of these frustrations, the first day back at school in September is always a happy one, and as I sit at my desk sorting through the cash I listen with delight to the first hymn of the shool year which echoes down the corridor from the Assembly Hall:

Glad that I live am I; that the sky is blue
Glad for the country lanes, and the fall of dew . . .

It is a good rousing start to the school year – and it's a melody I can't help joining in with as I pick out the Spanish pesetas, French centimes, American cents, Italian lire and Afghanistan wotsits that always turn up in the dinner money on this particular day.

CHAPTER THREE

Of the Community – For the Community

Community education enthusiasts consider that school premises which open 9.00 a.m. to 4.00 p.m. five days a week (term time only) for the education of children are feeble establishments that are not playing a full and proper role within society. When St. Cuthbert's merged with St. Claude's in the 1960s the Headmaster of the time shared these views and he decided that the new and enlarged St. Claude's should be a Community School. This ideal of the community school was in keeping with the progressive mood of the times, and the Headmaster stayed long enough to see his new venture launched – then moved to a larger (traditional) school. Successive Headteachers have modified, or expanded, the original community-school concept and during the time that Mr Masterton has been with us he has introduced a few service-to-the-community ideas of his own.

And so it is that you will find St. Claude's ablaze with light and in use most evenings, Saturday mornings, occasionally on Sundays and often during the school holidays. We have an After-School Club (for those children whose mothers go out to work), regular (and irregular) 'lettings' – more about these later – an afternoon Old Age Pensioner's Club, an evening Youth Club and a Holiday School. These activities receive well-meaning but erratic support by some parents, lukewarm support by most staff, and regular attention from The Press. They are not, however, regarded with much enthusiasm by Mr Potts and his small team of cleaners. But I suppose one of Mr

Masterton's most controversial innovations is his use of parents in the classroom.

Many Headteachers like to keep parents in their place, i.e. in the Headteacher's study (if they have something they wish to discuss), outside on the pavement waiting for their children (if they haven't), or sitting in the Assembly Hall giving vociferous (and hopefully financial) support at the times of Festivals and Dramatic Performances. They are allowed free range of the school (including the classrooms) only on 'open evenings' when they are expected to turn out loyally (whatever the weather), ask intelligent and pertinent questions, and then go home quietly when the class teacher indicates that she/he's had enough (usually by piling books into briefcase, locking desk and saying hearty things like '. . . and don't forget Mrs Fanshaw, you can pop in any time you like to discuss Lucy's work, if anything's worrying you').

I once worked for a Headteacher who normally allowed parents no further into the school than the office except when he wanted a working party of mothers to come in and do useful work. He would send out a note of appeal, then form a team of volunteers (who were always forthcoming) and set up a trestle table and chairs in a passageway outside the boiler room where, by the light of one dingy electric lamp, dutiful mums would slave away repairing library books, cutting out paper for Christmas decorations, or sewing up pantomime costumes. At afternoon playtime I would take them down a tray of tea and biscuits, and at the end of the day the Head would award them a dazzling smile and grateful thanks. During the course of their afternoon's work they would have heard the tramp of children's feet overhead and the distant yells from the playground. But they would have *seen* nothing of normal school afternoon activities – and they weren't allowed anywhere near the staffroom. It's not like this at St. Claude's.

At St. Claude's you will find parents everywhere. You will find them joining in with Assembly in the morning, queuing up to use the staff toilet in the afternoon, and you will find them using the office as a dumping place for babes-in-arms, heavy shopping and handbags. You will also find them in the staffroom. Whilst it's nice and friendly to see the mothers using the school like a second home, it's a bit of a nuisance when they come and join us in the staffroom for morning coffee and afternoon tea. I had been at St. Claude's for nearly six months before I remembered to look carefully around the staffroom before opening my mouth, and I shall never forget that embarrassing occasion when I burst in one morning playtime exclaiming, 'That Townsend girl stinks like a polecat today. I'm sure her knickers haven't been changed for months!' only to find myself facing the slowly reddening features of Mrs Townsend who was helping herself to a cup of coffee behind the counter. Then there was that unfortunate time when I warned the assembled staff that the entire James family were crawling alive with headlice – Mrs James having spent the last week having it off with an itinerant Right-To-Work marcher who was camping out at the James' place. Too late I noticed Mrs James' neighbour sitting in the corner of the room almost choking in her teacup with malicious delight. However, staffroom incidents notwithstanding, it is in the classroom (and, occasionally, the office) that the St. Claude's parents make a useful contribution to the school.

We all use them. Mrs Snow, who has 30 little ones between the ages of $4\frac{1}{2}$ and $5\frac{1}{2}$ – some of whom cannot put on their shoes or button up trousers without assistance – is very grateful when a parent comes in to offer help. If ten children can be taken away to a corner of the room to splodge paint on paper under the watchful eye of a parent, then the remaining twenty others can be taken, individually, through their reading exercises by Mrs Snow. Miss Krantz feels a little uneasy with parents in the classroom, but she is very glad of their assistance when the class goes swimming, or for a walk to 'study nature' on The Hill. Mr Singleton thinks that most parents are a nuisance, and he certainly won't have them in the classroom, but he is glad to make use of the musical talents of Fiona Harrow's mother who comes in twice a week to take the Early Music Group through their repertoire in the Music Room.

Mr Appleby has two mothers coming in regularly to supervise groups of children at needlework and cookery, Mr Masterton has organised a team of mothers to run the school library, and *I* will find a job for any parent who offers her or his assistance in the office – even if it's only sorting out the jumble cupboard. But it is Mr Scott who is the most enthusiastic supporter of parental involvement; he uses them every day. On one afternoon last week when one mother was taking a group of Mr Scott's girls at netball, and another was in the staffroom cooking biscuits, I had occasion to go into Mr Scott's classroom to query an entry in his dinner register. A third mother was supervising a mixed group of knitters, and the remaining children were plugged into headphones, with their eyes cast down upon their work cards. A purposeful buzz filled the room, and Mr. Scott, seated at his desk, appeared to be absorbed in a pile of exercise books. As I approached with the dinner register he looked up with a grin. He was reading the *Guardian*.

Of course a large number of the St. Claude's parents rarely come near the school; it's always the same small group of mothers who come to help term after term. Their motives are mixed. I think a few of them are frustrated teachers at heart and love to be left in charge of a group of children; others, who have talents or skills to offer, find satisfaction and self-expression in guiding the children's hands and interests. A couple of the wealthy ones come, I think, because they are bored at home, and one Mum who is having trouble with her marriage tells me that being involved in school life helps her to forget. Another one, who claims she is suffering from Psychosomatic Anxiety and has reached a 'personality crisis' in her life, says that contact with the children helps to give her a more balanced outlook. There is no doubt that Mr Masterton's 'community classroom' concept is of great benefit to all teachers and some parents. I'm not sure what good it does the children.

Two activities at St. Claude's that receive a lot of attention from The Press and the local radio station are the After-School Club, and the Holiday School.

The After-School Club was Mrs Henderson's idea. Mrs Henderson has two little girls (twins) in Mrs Snow's class and she is one of Mrs Snow's most reliable class helpers. Mrs Henderson was a Social Worker before her marriage and she approached Mr Masterton with her idea of the After-School Club because she was concerned about the safety of children whose mothers went out to work. 'I sometimes see the children playing around the dockside, or racing across the mainroad opposite the Council flats,' she said, 'it's really rather worrying.' Mrs Henderson's idea was that she would form a rota of mothers who would be willing to stay at school until, say, 5.45 p.m. to supervise a group of children in 'interesting activities'. If Mr Masterton liked the idea, could he make available the school hall, and maybe provide paper and crayons or paints, etc. for the children? Mrs Henderson suggested that parents who wanted their children to attend the After-School Club should be asked to contribute 30p daily which could cover the cost of refreshments, such as some orange squash and biscuits. Mr Masterton thought it was an excellent idea and sent out a note to all parents telling them about the new scheme.

For a while everything went well. But then certain mums on Mrs Henderson's rota found it inconvenient to put in attendance regularly and Mrs Henderson found that she was doing most of the supervising herself. Then, on a couple of occasions, we were let down completely. The person on duty didn't turn up. The first time this happened Mrs Snow volunteered to stay behind (and made sure that Mrs Henderson realised what a generous gesture this was – Mrs Snow living so far away from school and having such a long journey home) – but she wasn't going to be so generous the second time.

On that occasion I didn't realise that something had gone wrong until Mr Potts came hurrying into the office just as I was packing up. 'There's ten children roaring around the hall,' he said, 'they're playing merry hell with the piano and no-one's looking after them.' I ran out into the playground and caught Mrs Snow and Miss Krantz just about to leave by the back gate. Mrs Snow, getting into her car quickly, said, 'I'm awfully sorry Helen, but I can't possibly stay; I've got a dental appointment.' Miss Krantz, grumbling that people-who-start-these-things-should-see-to-it-that-they-are-run-properly, reluctantly agreed to take over.

Mr Masterton and Mrs Henderson had an urgent meeting the next day. Neither wanted the After-School Club to fold up, and it was felt that if the scheme were operated on a sounder financial basis they could actually afford to employ someone to do the job. So they doubled the charge to parents and then placed an advertisement in the local Post Office – hoping to interest an out-of-work young teacher.

The employed playleader project for the After-School Club got off to a bad start. The first girl employed to do the job stayed for two days and then told Mrs Henderson that she couldn't stand it any more. (The first evening she lost two children who took off down to the sweet shop and didn't come back – and during the second evening the Crombie twins let down the tyres of her bicycle.) Then a young man was appointed. He managed the job very well; the children were disciplined and happily occupied. He was with us for three weeks and then disappeared – with him went a large tin of biscuits, the evening's takings of £6.30 and one of Mr Singleton's guitars. Then they appointed the present young lady who has been happily running the After-School Club for about eight months.

Mr Potts complains about the orange squash slopped on the floor, the biscuits and abandoned crisp packets he finds stuffed behind the radiators and the scattered paint brushes and sheets of paper he has to remove each evening, but Mrs Henderson is now glad that her scheme is running smoothly. However, on my way home from school last Friday I noticed several of the youngsters from the Council flats racing across the main road, obviously intent on a few hours' play in the area of abandoned warehouses alongside the old docks. Certainly the nine children who were staying to the After-School Club that afternoon all had working mothers – amongst them two secondary-school teachers, one gynaecological consultant, two civil servants and a librarian. All these parents are extremely glad that the St. Claude's After-School Club exists. I don't suppose, however, that they are the mums Mrs Henderson had in mind when she created it.

The St. Claude's Holiday School was the joint idea of Mr Masterton and Mrs Glugburn (Chairman of our Governors). They both felt very strongly that it was wrong for St. Claude's to stay shut for six weeks during the summer whilst the children of local working people ran wild in the streets. Mrs Glugburn is a very persuasive and forceful woman and she persuaded the Local Authority

44

not only to set aside an amount of money each year to equip the St. Claude's Holiday School, but also to create a 3-week teaching post (open to any teacher employed in the County). The person who is appointed for this 3-week vacational job receives extra pay and is given the authority to appoint up to four paid helpers. So far each year a different teacher has taken on the job of running the St. Claude's Holiday School; and so far none of the teaching staff at St. Claude's has applied for it. As I am never at the school when the St. Claude's Holiday School is in operation I can't really say what happens; I only know about the careful preparations we all make for it. On the last day of the summer term each member of staff puts away all books, pencils, paint and paper and locks all cupboard doors. Sports equipment and musical instruments are piled into the stock cupboard, and I take my typewriter, duplicators and copying machine into Mr Masterton's office – the door of which stays locked throughout the holiday. I understand that the children attending the Holiday School are occupied with pottery, carpentry and artwork and that outings are arranged to local places of interest.

Mr Potts finds it difficult to accept the existence of the Holiday School with his usual phlegm and is, I think, envious of other school caretakers who have the whole six weeks summer holiday in which to take their own holidays and to clean and polish the school ready for the autumn term, whilst he has to make do with just half of that time. And whereas he accepts that lavatory pans blocked by toilet rolls, windows broken by footballs, and woodwork scarred by sheath knives are all part of normal school life, the damage inflicted upon St. Claude's by the Holiday School never fails to jar even his unflappable disposition and to invoke his wrath against the organisers. It seems to me that people who choose to volunteer their services to run Holiday Schools could be classed as 'Sensitive Community-conscious Progressives', or 'Bloody Hopeless Half-Wits' – depending upon whether the classifier is a socially-minded educationalist, or a school caretaker.

The Holiday School is certainly well supported. It is not limited to the children of St. Claude's and during the weeks before the end of the summer term I receive calls from parents all over the city asking for information about it. Each August anything up to 60 children will come along to St. Claude's, and there is always a cheerful picture published in the local paper showing children in the playground larking about happily on the equipment under the supervision of an enthusiastic helper. Some of the children are ours.

Another scheme which is unique (I believe) to St. Claude's is our accommodation of YOBs ('students' from the Young Offenders' Bureau).

I think it was about six years ago that a social worker involved with the Young Offenders' Bureau first contacted St. Claude's with a view to placing one of their young probationers at our school for a period of training and rehabilitation. The idea was that some young person who had become involved in Police Court proceedings could, by daily work within the innocent and totally unbiased community of a state primary school, be persuaded to take a responsible attitude to life in general and to mend his ways. It was stressed by the social worker that no offender with a record of sexual offences or physical violence would be considered for such a scheme. Mr Masterton was intrigued by the idea, and put it to the next meeting of the Parents and Teachers' Association. I remember that at that time we had on our PTA a plethora of sociologists, educational psychologists and probation officers – and the scheme was wholeheartedly endorsed.

Ever since then we have, each term, accommodated a YOB student in the 'classroom situation' at St. Claude's. But times change. The children of six years ago have now left us for secondary school, and the sociologists, educational psychologists and probation officers are now vociferously making their feelings known at PTA meetings further up the educational ladder. The St. Claude's PTA committee this year consists of a few employees of the local council, an architect, someone involved in local radio and a man connected with the electronics industry. Their views on the presence of YOB students in the classroom are not known (they probably don't even know of the scheme's existence); the item has never since appeared on the agenda. We are much more concerned these days with the faulty electrics in the swimming pool, the appalling decorative state of the school, and the arguments for and against the purchase of a school mini-bus. And as many students these days wear dirty jeans, earrings and multi-coloured hair, the YOB student mingles unnoticed with those from the university or polytechnic who come to do periods of training with us from time to time.

The YOB student normally works with Mr Appleby's class and helps out with the supervision of games, swimming, carpentry and model making. Some of them have been very friendly, affable and helpful young men who have stayed with us several weeks before disappearing. (When the YOB student goes missing for more than two days I know that I shall shortly receive a telephone call from the Bureau informing me that 'unfortunately Michael borrowed a car without asking the owner's permission and is now back in Borstal' – or something similar.) Sometimes the YOB student is uncommunicative and ill-at-ease; such students usually only stay with us a couple of days, and spend most of their time at school skulking in the staffroom. I once saw a surly YOB heavyweight being accosted by a tiny six-year-old girl in the corridor who was demanding to know, with a smile and pointing forefinger, why the youth was wearing a pin in his ear. I am sure that such a query from an adult would have earned a raised fist, but confronted by such charming innocence the gorilla blushed, stammered, and edged his way unanswering past her into the staffroom.

With such an assortment of students and parents in the school, a visitor to the staffroom at coffee time would be foolish to assume that the person he is sitting next to has an academic background. The situation has become further complicated since the advent of the Youth Opportunities Programme which means that, more often than not, we have a YOP student as well as a YOB. The visitor who politely enquires of the young student sitting alongside him 'And where did you do your training?' is liable to get a totally unexpected answer.

Religion, at St. Claude's, is a very delicate matter. The original Victorian church of St. Claude's was de-consecrated in the 1950s (and is now a tyre warehouse) and the school now has no affiliation with any religious establishment. Many of our parents appear not to feel strongly about religion, but quite a number of them (particularly amongst Types 1 and 4) would, I know, feel hurt and worried if the school didn't occasionally observe some form of Christian ritual. On the other hand a vociferous and articulate group of non-believers (mostly Type 2) protest strongly at anything in the school curriculum which they feel smacks of orthodox religious indoctrination. (One Christmas, when the staff were trying to decide what gifts our Father Christmas should distribute, Mr Singleton – after a quick look around the staffroom to make sure that no parents were there – sardonically suggested that each child be presented with a bible. We all burst out laughing at such a preposterous idea.) Mr Masterton manages to tread a very carefully balanced path between these opposing views of the parents by conducting a daily Assembly which has a moral, but not a religious, message – and then having good rousing Christian celebrations on the occasions of Easter, Harvest Festival and Christmas.

The St. Claude's reputation for liberal and all-embracing attitudes may be responsible for the fact that the people who book our premises for their meetings – (these occasions are known as 'lettings') – are very different from those who book elsewhere. Whereas our nearest neighbouring school (Commercial Street J.M. & I.) gets the Brownies, the Ladies' Flower Arranging Group, and occasionally the Social Democrats, we are landed with WOW (Wider Opportunities for Women); WAR (Women Against Rape); SPAT (Society for the Prevention of Animal Trapping), and the CND. Many of these people cause great worry to Mr Potts who has to let them in, somehow get them out again, and then clear up afterwards. He once had to cope with a group calling themselves MAWR (which I first took to be a Welsh extremist organisation but it turned out to be some strange men wearing long gowns and sandals claiming that they were Men Against Women's Rights) – who had booked the school hall for Saturday evening and Sunday morning. Mr Potts had told me of his worries on the Friday prior to their visit. 'Where are they going to spend Saturday night? . . . That's what I want to know!' he said. On that occasion Mr Potts' worries turned out to be prophetic. He was obliged

48

to call the police at midnight in order to assist him turf out the assembled brotherhood who were getting out sleeping bags and lighting camping stoves all around the school hall.

Mr Masterton can justifiably claim that the doors of St. Claude's are rarely locked during the day and evening and that no-one is refused entry. Mothers bring their neuroses and marriage problems to school along with their children; students who are 'into' peace movements, ecology, or world famine, swamp us with letters of application to do their post-graduate training with us; welfare organisations come and observe us; teachers from other schools who want to know more about community education come to study with us, foreigners of all colours and creeds visit us . . . and lady editors of newspaper 'Women's Pages' love us. Mr Masterton is, quite rightly, well-known and highly regarded; and I have even heard it whispered that he might be lined up for an OBE next year. But whilst agreeing that Mr Masterton's hard work and idealistic ventures ought to receive recognition, perhaps it is Mr Potts who should get the medal.

CHAPTER FOUR

The Staff . . . and Me

'But what do you actually *do*?' is a question I am
sometimes asked by people who haven't seen the inside of
a primary school since the day they left one as a child. They
know that I start work at 8.45 each morning and leave at
4.00 in the afternoon and have all school holidays to
myself. They obviously believe that I have an enviable and
leisurely post and they are puzzled about what happens in
the school office when classes are in session. As there isn't
such a thing as a 'typical' day to describe, I usually just
shrug my shoulders, wave my hands and say vague things
like 'Oh! – anything and everything'. Hidden somewhere
at the back of my filing cabinet is an official document
which came from The Authority a few years ago and which
lists the duties to be expected of a school secretary. When
this document arrived I read it in horror and took great
pains to ensure that Mr Masterton didn't set eyes upon it,
because the thing gave him a 'carte' even more 'blanche'
than he suspected.

The list contained things I do as routine (like counting
dinner money, keeping records, typing letters, checking
invoices, filing, and completing forms); also things I
should do as routine but rarely get around to (like checking
the teachers' attendance registers each week and striking a
balance on the School Fund account); and it finished with
the item . . . 'and any other duty that the Headteacher may
request'. Under this heading would come the bloody knees
I bandage, the footballs I retrieve from roof gutterings; the
toilet rolls I remove with an old ruler from blocked

lavatory pans, and the lies I put down on our annual statistical return of class sizes.* I do all these things cheerfully, and earn Mr Masterton's gratitude. If he knew about that final item in the document on the Official Duties of School Secretaries, he wouldn't feel the need to be so grateful – and he'd probably think up a few more for me.

I can remember my first day as a primary school secretary. I was extremely nervous. I had come from working in a large, friendly typing pool where, during the lunch break, the girls knitted pullovers for their boyfriends and read *Women's Weekly*. Their general conversation was about the programme on TV last night; where they were going for their holidays; and the super little restaurant they discovered last weekend. I was now working as the only clerical assistant on a staff of professional academics; if I were allowed access to the staffroom I would probably have to sit humbly and hold my tongue. As it turned out I found I had been worrying unnecessarily. True, my colleagues at school prefer the *Guardian* to *Women's Weekly* and go in for macramé-worked holdalls rather than knitted pullovers – but the general talk in the staffroom centres on what was on TV last night; where they are going for their holidays; and the super little restaurant they discovered last weekend.

Another surprising thing I found out was that I am not the only member of staff with this sense of 'aloneness'. We are all individuals; each of us has a separate task to perform in this school – and if you think that the teacher of Class 1 has pretty much the same job as the teacher of Class 5 then you would be wrong. Mrs Snow would be terrified at the thought of taking Mr Appleby's roughnecks for a session,

---

* The number of 'teaching hours' allocated to a school is dependent upon the number of pupils on roll. Any drop in numbers, therefore, means that some teaching hours, or even a teaching post, may be taken away from the school – and it is upon the figures submitted in the Annual Return that the decisions are made. The Annual Return applies to one day only, specified by The Authority. If any children leave St. Claude's to go abroad, or to another LEA area during the couple of months prior to the date of the Annual Return, I delay notifying The Authority of this fact, and leave the children 'on roll' until the day after the Return. We then hope that in the succeeding year we can make up these lost numbers before the date of the next Annual Return.

and Mr Appleby doesn't like to go near Mrs Snow's reception class – he's frightened of stepping on one of them.

Some schools manage to maintain a uniform feeling between each class, but this only happens if the Head imposes his or her views upon the curriculum. Some Heads decide that a certain Maths Scheme and Literacy Scheme shall be followed throughout the school, and the teachers must conform. Some Heads even insist that each teacher keeps a diary or log book – noting down aims and objectives of lessons, and detailing future plans. But it's not like that at St. Claude's. Mr Masterton believes that children will learn more if the teachers in charge of them are happy; and the teachers in charge can only be happy if they are left alone to follow personal choices of teaching methods. Mr Masterton sees his role as keeping a fatherly eye upon the welfare of staff and children alike; I see my role as giving a helping hand to any member of staff who needs it. Their demands on me are various and curious, and if you'll come with me around the classes I will explain what I mean. Let's start in the infant's department.

Mrs Snow's reception class is pink and cosy. The walls are covered with happy, friendly pictures and fluffy, pastel collages that change with the seasons throughout the year. The pink hearts and lace of Valentine's day will be replaced by pussy willows and woolly lambs – to be followed by fluffy yellow chicks at Easter time. Mrs Snow, who is skilled with scissors, paint and paper, surrounds her children with a changing pattern of soft colours and restful concepts. Mrs Snow believes that children should learn through play. She has a Wendy House, complete with mini kitchen (plates, cups, saucepans and a stove) and a mini lounge (TV, telephone handset and books). She has a sand pit, a farm, a castle and a Book Corner and at all times of the day you will find children distributed about her room learning through play.

'Mathematics' is a favourite game. 'Mathematics' means lots of colourful plastic shapes (contained in boxes with names like 'Dog and Bone', 'Insey Winsey Spider' and 'Greedy Grub'), but the most popular Mathematical task seems to be sorting through a pack of cards labelled 'Scaredy Cat'. This sends the children into shrieks of excitement every time the 'Scaredy Cat' joker card comes up amongst the unsuspecting pretty little birds painted in ones and twos on the rest of the cards. What surprises me is the amount of shape identification (we used to call it Geometry) that is considered so important in infant 'mathematics' these days. When Mrs Snow's children move up into the next class most of them can tell 5 'scaredy cat' birds from 7, and with crayons grasped in chubby little fingers, they can draw and recognise cuboids, cylinders, cones, spheres and rhomboids. Mrs Snow loves children, and at any time of the day you can go into her classroom and find her seated upon a pile of cushions on the floor, surrounded by paper, books and children. Several will be fighting for a place upon her lap, whilst two more hang around her neck.

I find that the only way I can help Mrs Snow is by attending to her personal phone calls. Mrs Snow has a large country house with a roof that leaks and a gas central heating system which is always going wrong. She is also having an extension built on to the north wing. As we all know, builders, plumbers and the Gas Board work from 10.00 a.m. to 3.00 p.m. Mondays to Fridays, take two hours for lunch and rarely answer the telephone. Mrs Snow has spent several playtimes, dinner times and after-school times trying (without success) to get hold of necessary workmen, and I don't in the least mind when she asks me . . . 'If you have a minute do you think you could try this number . . . ' If I go into Mrs Snow's classroom mid-afternoon, disentangle her from cushions and children and pass on the message that Harry Crump has got hold of the pantiles you wanted and will be round on Thursday morning definite to fix them – the smile of relief on her face is all the reassurance I need that Mrs Snow's demanding day has been made that much easier by a little effort on my part.

When the children move up from Mrs Snow's class into Miss Krantz's we have a few problems with complaints of wet knickers, obscure tummy disorders, and worried bewildered Mums who come to the office and wail that their little girl used to be so happy at the thought of coming to school but now she is in tears every morning. It usually takes about half a term for the children to settle down and learn to cope with Miss Krantz's teaching methods, which are entirely different from those of Mrs Snow.

Miss Krantz has many strong views. She expresses these views frequently. In a loud voice. Miss Krantz thinks that money should not be wasted on unnecessary equipment . . . 'THE ONLY MATHS EQUIPMENT MY CHILDREN NEED IS A PENCIL AND PAPER'. Miss Krantz likes a quiet and orderly classroom . . . 'A CHILD'S ATTITUDE TO SELF-DISCIPLINE SHOULD BE ESTABLISHED AT THE INFANT STAGE' . . . and she makes her children sit at little tables lined up in rows. If a child chatters in class, it must sit with its finger held to its lips for five minutes. If a child misbehaves in class it will have to spend playtime standing outside the staffroom door with its hands clasped upon its head. Miss Krantz doesn't believe in wall displays . . . 'THE ONLY ARTWORK YOU WILL SEE UPON MY WALLS IS WHAT THE CHILDREN HAVE DONE THEMSELVES' . . . Miss Krantz feels that sexist attitudes should not be encouraged in the children . . . 'HOW CAN THEY GROW UP FEELING EQUAL IF THEIR DIFFERENCES ARE EMPHASISED AT THIS AGE?' . . . and she has abandoned Mrs Snow's 'John and Mary' reading scheme because it shows pictures of John helping Daddy in the garage and Mary helping Mummy in the kitchen. Little girls are discouraged from wearing frilly dresses and jewellery, and they are not allowed to bring their dollies to school. The daily task of arranging flowers or twigs in the 'Nature Corner' is usually given to little boys – and *they* are not allowed to bring toy cars to school.

Miss Krantz has a lot of personal problems. She lives with her elderly and ailing mother in a crumbling old town house. The house has a gable-end which is cracked, drains which are often blocked, and neighbours who are noisy. Miss Krantz suffers with occasional dizzy spells and varicose veins. When the job of Deputy Head became vacant at St. Claude's Miss Krantz applied for it – but was passed over in favour of Mr Appleby, who is six years her junior. Sometimes, usually around mid-morning, when Miss Krantz has her class quietly settled at their work, she will come to the office to talk. At first I used to give thought to Miss Krantz's problems and try to make helpful suggestions. But she didn't really want to listen. Any comment of mine would be swept away with a remark like 'AH YES, BUT . . .' and she would go on to tell me of further complications. So now I just let her talk. I realise that all Miss Krantz requires of the school secretary is a sympathetic ear. I keep a friendly-helpful expression upon my face as I carry on adding up columns of figures, and every now and then I give a friendly-helpful nod of the head. After a while Miss Krantz gives a big sigh and then heaves herself out of her chair saying, 'I'D BETTER LET YOU GET ON WITH YOUR WORK HADN'T I?' . . . and she trudges off to her classroom.

When the children leave Miss Krantz's class to further their education with Mr Scott they are usually polite, docile, and most of them wear trousers. The majority of them will be able to read simple sentences (having all reached the same stage in the XYZ Reading Series) and they will be able to add up and subtract figures (having all reached the same stage in the 789 Maths Series).

The first thing that bewilders the children on entering Mr Scott's classroom is the fact that there are no lines of tables. There aren't many chairs either. But there are lots and lots of big cushions, a television set, several radio-cassette players, lots of headphones, a film projector, an overhead slide projector, and rack after rack of floor jigsaw puzzles, Parquetry Plus sets, Pig-in-the-Middle spelling games, Mathematical Flipover Logiblocs, Bulmershe Mathematical Activity cards, Beefeater Height Measure Stands, Trundle Wheels, Equaliser Balance sets, and a large, rather mucky, overflowing clay bin. It's like Mrs Snow's all over again, but a bit more technical.

The walls are covered with posters exhorting the children to Clean Their Teeth, Watch out for Cars, Identify Birds of Estuary and Forest, and Maintain their Bicycles. Mr Scott loves posters. He doesn't mind what they say, so long as they say it in bright bold letters and bright bold pictures. Any posters that come to the school are automatically passed to Mr Scott to pin up on his walls. The latest one encourages his children to Think European and illustrates various cheeses that are now selling abroad. Derbyshire, Cheddar, Gloucester, Wensleydale and

Caerphilly cheeses are pictured over a slogan which reads 'You can always distinguish *English*'. When I pointed out to him the gross territorial error he pushed me out of the room with a laugh and a familiar pat on the bottom. 'You're too fussy,' he said, 'and anyway, they never look at the bloody things.'

Mr Scott keeps me busy duplicating worksheets. These worksheets come as tear-off pages in books with titles like 'Traffic in Town and Country', 'The River from Source to Mouth', or 'The Norman Conquest in England' – they are printed in heavy carbon all ready for duplication on a spirit duplicator, and I turn out about 35 copies daily for Mr Scott's class. Each worksheet carries a line-drawn illustration, a few sentences of explanatory text, and then a list of questions to be answered. Sometimes the questions are undemanding. The child is required merely to tick the correct box. (For example 'The soldier in the front of the picture has a weapon in his hand. Is it (A) a long bow (B) a sword (C) a crossbow (D) a sabre'?) On other occasions the questions are meant to stimulate the imagination and call for a full answer. (For example 'The woman standing on the corner of the pavement looks very worried. What do you think she is thinking about?')

The children love the worksheets almost as much as Mr Scott does. Those with original thoughts write many pages – happily uninterrupted, and cheerfully slapdash about spelling. (Any careful child who insists upon being told the correct way of spelling a word will be sent down to me . . . 'Mr Scott says will you please tell me how many "lls" there are in channelled?' . . . because Mr Scott is also slapdash about spelling.) A child who can't understand the printed text, let alone form any answers, will amuse itself by colouring in the drawing. Mr Scott doesn't mind – just so long as they are quiet, with their heads down, whilst he fiddles with a jammed cassette tape, or rummages around in an overflowing cupboard looking for a film strip, or even perhaps sorts out his register. (Mr Scott normally fills in only the noughts in his register – indicating absences – leaving it several weeks before he completes all the strokes – indicating children present – and adds it up. Last year he got to the end of one term and found he had lost a week somewhere, and I had to issue him with a new register to re-write.)

Sometimes Mr Scott's worksheets are pleasantly illustrated and have stimulating texts. Others are crude and misleading. A pile I took in to him recently depicted a roughly drawn oystercatcher and bore the information, 'This bird is called an oystercatcher because it eats oysters. It uses its long beak to prise open the oyster shells in the same way that you would lever open a tin with a chisel.' As I dumped the pile on his desk I told him that I didn't think the oystercatchers at present pottering about on our river mudflats would know an oyster if they saw one . . . and what about the molluscs, worms, insects and other crustacea that formed their normal diet? I also told Mr Scott, as I backed away, that if fathers knew that their children were being encouraged to open tins with chisels they would, quite justifiably, be furious. I then got out of the room quickly. I think Mr Scott was about to throw a book at me.

Apart from the daily twenty minutes when they are all busy with their worksheets, Mr Scott's children are normally split into various groups – all following different activities. Thus, when entering his room, you could find a group of children seated in front of the T.V. set, totally absorbed in the 'Maths with Laughs' series, whilst others are attached to earphones following the 'India, village life and crafts' geography project on the radio. Some children will be up to their elbows in clay at the pottery bench, while a few more will be spreadeagled amongst the plastic Lego or coloured counters on the floor. There is always a cheerful buzz in Mr Scott's classroom, and quite a lot of laughter. Once a week, on Wednesday mornings, all group activities are abandoned for twenty minutes when the class tunes into the radio broadcast of Singing Together – and Mr Scott, sitting cross-legged upon his desk, sings loudest of all.

The children bring in pieces of cake for Mr Scott on their birthdays, and they make him birthday cards when it is his. All the little girls love Mr Scott, and there are often tears when the time comes for them to move up into Mr Singleton's class.

Mr Singleton considers that his classroom is an oasis of calm and order in a school of noise and confusion. He is at heart a very kind man, but to the children who come tumbling cheerfully into his class from Mr Scott's room he presents a stern and intimidating demeanour. This is a deliberate policy of his. 'Start off as you mean to go on' is his maxim, and he wishes to impress on these newcomers that their days of sprawling on the floor and scribbling rubbish on bits of paper are over. Mr Singleton knows that he is regarded with terror by the infants, and it is an image that he doesn't wish to dispel. Once, when I asked an infant to take a message up to Mrs Beagle in the kitchen, the child gazed at me in horror. 'But that means passing Mr Singleton's room,' she whispered. She obviously had visions of Mr Singleton, darting out like a scrawny brown spider, to grab at her as she crept along the corridor outside his room.

The general colour tone in Mr Singleton's room is a restful sepia, or a depressing sludge-brown, depending upon your point of view. There *are* some pictures on the wall. Mr Singleton has nine of them – all properly framed and glazed – and he displays three of them each term in sequence. A green woodland scene entitled 'What to look for in Spring' will be followed by a pink-blossomed woodland scene entitled 'What to look for in Summer' to be followed by . . . (but I don't need to tell you the rest). Mr Singleton sees no reason for changing his sets of pictures as they will all be fresh to each succeeding year's class.

Mr Singleton's room is filled with neat lines of polished brown oak desks, and he has two large pitch-pine cupboards. We all think this furniture dates from the day when the school was opened last century – one of the desks has the date 1911 carved into it – and Mr Singleton sees no reason why it shouldn't all last for another century. Not long ago The Authority notified us that we were entitled to a Furniture Renewal Allowance and invited us to refurbish our classrooms as we thought fit. A young lady from The Authority visited us with catalogues and Mr Masterton suggested that each teacher should choose a new set of furniture. I can remember that the catalogues were passed around the staffroom and were enthusiastically thumbed through by every member of staff, except Mr Singleton who insisted that there was nothing wrong with the furniture at present in his room.

Mr Singleton's fuddy-duddy attitude towards the new

furniture was sniggered at by the rest of the staff, but I rather think that he has had the last laugh. The new grey moulded plastic chairs may have pretty colour-coded plastic trim on the legs to indicate the age of child to be accommodated, but they are so light in weight that they can be flung across the room with ease, and usually split when they hit the wall. The tall grey plastic bookshelf units fall over if heavy books are put on the top shelf, and the side panels crack when kicked. The drawer units look very smart and modern with their removable plastic trays that slide into the unit along moulded plastic ridges – but if the trays are more than half-filled with items they fall off their runners. (Miss Krantz became disenchanted with her drawer units on the first day, and as all the discarded shabby wooden furniture was still stacked in the playground awaiting collection by The Authority's Furniture Disposal Department, she persuaded Mr Potts to drag back into her classroom one of her old cupboards.)

Mr Singleton's attitude to new furniture is echoed by his attitude to new methods, commercially produced Maths Schemes and Reading Schemes, audio-visual equipment, or any form of 'teaching aid' with the exception of chalk, a blackboard pointer and a set of maps. Mr Singleton keeps his children sitting at their desks and following a strict timetable of work which includes all the traditional subjects and, surprisingly, class discussion groups. They also recite multiplication tables. (This used to worry Mr Masterton in the early 'freedom of expression' days and he would go out of his way to avoid taking prospective parents past Mr Singleton's room. But now that the 'back to basics' move is well established he is proud to draw attention to the rhythmic (and totally accurate) chant coming from the class. 'Nothing like the old methods' he will say, inclining his head with a whimsical smile as he ushers parents along the corridor.)

Mr Singleton takes his class for four outings during the year (once to the Museum, and three, in season, around The Hill) and is generally cynical about present educational standards which he considers are going from bad to worse. He sees one hopeful sign only – and this is the renewed interest in the musical instruments, songs and tunes of mediaeval England. The St. Claude's Early Music

Group was Mr Singleton's idea, and its remarkable achievements are entirely due to the enthusiasm and hard work of the young players under his encouragement and direction.

Mr Singleton asks very little of me, but as he is in charge of music he occasionally asks me to type and duplicate hymnsheets for Easter, Harvest Festival and Christmas. (After each musical occasion he carefully collects all the sheets back from the children to keep until next year, so it is only if he decides upon a change of hymn, or if the sheets become too dog-eared, that he calls for my assistance.) Occasionally he will ask me to photocopy some sheet music for his Early Music Group. The first time he did this I jokingly referred to the Copyright Act (all schools regard the Copyright Act as a joke) and asked him how he thought poor struggling composers would manage if everyone photocopied their work. Mr Singleton said that as this particular poor struggling composer had been dead for 500 years the point was irrelevant, but a few months passed before he asked me, somewhat sheepishly, to do some more. (I rather think his diffidence has more to do with not wanting to admit to having any use for a photocopier than any worries about infringing the Copyright Act. Needless to say, neither of us is the least bit concerned about the poor struggling publisher.)

At the age of 9+ the children move up to Mr Appleby's class for their final year or 18 months at St. Claude's. I think they go with mixed feelings. They knew where they were in Mr Singleton's class. They knew what was required of them. For a year they had been surrounded by the homely security of a daily pattern of work; some of them even admit to a grudging affection for old Sing-Song-Singey. He had made many demands of them. He had demanded that they should be disciplined and attentive. He demanded that they should work hard and express themselves thoughtfully and carefully. Each child had responded to the best of its ability. But now new, and much tougher, demands are going to be made of them. Mr Appleby demands that each child should 'discover its identity'.

Mr Appleby sees his role as encouraging the children to 'blossom' in self-fulfilment. Mr Appleby's 'blossoms' usually fall into two groups; those who soon find their identity and become the bully-boys and bossy-girls flexing their wits, and ready to take on the demands of secondary school – and those who don't. Mr Appleby has no set timetable. Each child chooses what it wants to do, and Mr Appleby moves from group to group, or child to child, helping out where necessary.

Mr Appleby is a wholehearted supporter of the Community School ideal. He is also totally opposed to the old-fashioned notion of separating the school ancillary workers from the teaching staff. (He once worked at a school where the secretary as well as the parents were banned from the staffroom. He described the atmosphere there as 'sterile and stultifying'.) Mr Appleby believes that all adults should be totally committed to the education of children. This means that his cookery classes are normally carried out in the staffroom (and we all have to crunch our way across sugar-laden floors and watch out for cake-mix upon chair seats) . . . his art classes take place with paint and glue on the floors, the walls, and the doors of his room (and Mr Potts spends nearly half of his cleaning time removing it) . . . and his physics experiments don't work without the intervention of the school secretary. Certainly – we are all totally involved in Mr Appleby's classes. (Even Mrs Beagle used to be, when he held his cookery classes in the kitchen during the afternoons. But when Mrs Beagle threatened to leave because of dough-encrusted dishcloths, bent spoons, distorted forks and tea towels that had been used to wipe the floor, Mr Appleby was persuaded to transfer the class to the staffroom.)

It is, perhaps, Mr Appleby who makes most use of the school secretary. When Mr Appleby holds a lino-cutting craft session it is me who applies plasters and sympathy to bleeding cuts. When Mr Appleby once placed a Ribena bottle filled with water in the fridge in order to demonstrate that water expands when it freezes, it was me who delicately bashed the bottle with a hammer in order to 'prove the point'. When Mr Appleby wished to prove that yeast feeds on glucose, it was me who 'doctored' the jug with several spoonfuls of sugar from the staff tea cupboard – in order to make the yeast respond frothily. When, from time to time, I suggest to Mr Appleby that such practices could be construed as deceit he looks hurt, and insists that I am merely helping to get the message over.

Mr Appleby's energy and enthusiasm knows no bounds. I shall never forget the mercury incident of last summer. One day just after school had started in the morning a mother came to the office carrying an old-fashioned looking bottle with a ground glass stopper. She held it out to me saying that it had been hanging around in a cupboard at home for a long time now and she was wondering if the school could make use of it. What she didn't say was that the bottle contained mercury. I held out my hand to take it and, being quite unprepared for the weight, I found the bottle slipping straight through my fingers. I fumbled in vain. The bottle crashed upon the office floor, spattering shards of glass and globules of mercury everywhere. The mother clutched her skirt around her knees with one hand, covered her mouth and nose with the other, and regarded me with an expression of horror in her eyes. 'But it's dangerous isn't it?' she mumbled from behind her hand. Danger notwithstanding, I persuaded her to stand guard over the mess on the floor whilst I went to get a brush and dustpan from Mr Pott's cupboard, and then she stood there (trying not to breathe) whilst I swept it up. When she eventually made her escape from the office we were both earnestly apologising to each other . . . and I was relieved that she had apparently not noticed the cluster of dusty globules that had eluded my brush and rolled behind the filing cabinet.

There is probably something laid down in the Health and Safety Regulations about mercury. Probably I should have notified The Authority, sent for the Fire Brigade and evacuated the school. Instead I took my rather weighty dustpan down to the boiler room, found one of Mr Potts' roof-leak-emergency buckets, and dumped the mess of glass and mercury into it. I knew that the problem couldn't end there. Somehow the contents of the bucket would have to be disposed of. It obviously shouldn't be put out into the school dustbins, and I toyed with the idea of persuading Mr Potts to sneak out onto The Hill at midnight to dig a hole and bury it, but when I later discussed the matter with Mr Appleby he wouldn't hear of it. He had apparently read of a method of cleaning mercury and separating it from all foreign matter. 'You mix it with sugar and squeeze it through chamois leather,' he said. 'You leave it to me; I'll sort it out. I could use that mercury in physics.' At the end of the afternoon I retrieved the bucket from the boiler house and took it to Mr Appleby who planned to 'sort it out' after school.

The first thing I noticed the next day was Mr Appleby coming into school with heavily bandaged hands. I decided that it would be tactful to refrain from comment. At morning coffee time it was discovered that all the staffroom sugar had disappeared. As none of the other staff had known anything about Mr Appleby's experiment I decided that it would be even more tactful to refrain from comment. But when an indignant Mr Potts came to the office bearing a bucket containing glass, mercury, and the tattered and blood-spattered remains of his best chamois leather, I felt that an explanation was called for. He took it stoically. Neither Mr Appleby nor I have referred to the mercury incident since; and I don't know what Mr Potts eventually did with the contents of the bucket. I decided that it was best not to ask.

We have now completed our tour of the classrooms and I hope you have some inkling of the sort of assistance I give to the teaching staff. So far as I am able to judge, the educational standards achieved at St. Claude's seem to be similar to those of other primary schools. But because of recent public misgivings about the scholastic attainments of secondary school-leavers (a sore point amongst employers – who blame the secondary schools – who blame the primary schools – who blame the nursery school – who blame the parents) there is, currently, a move towards more co-operation between primary schools and secondary schools in order to counter criticisms that the educational needs of the young are being neglected. Mr Masterton, who has a natural instinct for current moves, wondered whether the numeracy of the St. Claude's children might be improved by the introduction throughout the school of something called 'Fletcher Maths'. He asked me to telephone our local secondary school to find out what they thought of this currently popular mathematics scheme. I spoke to the Head of Maths. He was not very cordial. 'We don't give a damn what scheme you follow,' he said (somewhat hysterically I thought) . . . 'just send them to us able to read, write, add up, subtract and multiply; that's all we ask!'

But whatever the local secondary school thinks about the educational standards achieved at St. Claude's, it is a fact that by the time our children have progressed through the stages from Mrs Snow's class to Mr Appleby's they will have learned one of life's most important lessons . . . that survival depends upon adaptability.

CHAPTER FIVE

The children ... and me

I am not at ease with children; I just don't respond to them automatically. When my nephews and nieces were small I can remember, on the rare occasions I visited them, being almost tongue-tied with embarrassment. In spite of rehearsing beforehand appropriate Auntie-like sentences to say to them, and deciding upon correct Auntie-like attitudes to adopt, I found myself blundering about with questions like 'And what do you enjoy doing at school' – which left us all totally bored and glad when the occasion was over. Now, if you dumped in my lap a lively puppy, an elderly cat, a tame sparrow, a sick hen, a bewildered lamb or even a goldfish I think I would establish immediate and sympathetic communication. But with children I am uneasy.

I didn't anticipate any problems on this score when becoming a school secretary because I couldn't foresee that there would be much contact between me and the pupils. The children, I thought, would hang up their clothes in the cloakroom in the morning – go into the classroom – play in the playground – eat in the dinner hall – and then collect their coats and go home at the end of the day. I was wrong. I discovered that not only were they in the office clamouring for attention before lessons started, during playtime, dinnertime, and when lessons were over, but that they were also sent to the office during lesson time if something was needed from the stock cupboard, or if they were not feeling very well, or if they had been naughty in class. (Children who break up chairs, swear at the teacher, refuse to work, or throw books across the classroom are sent down to stand outside Mr Masterton's office. Which means they stand in mine.)

It took me about six weeks to come to terms with the fact that children are an unavoidable part of school life, and I now stoically accept children who lean breathily over my desk, crawl about under my feet, drum their heels against the wall, swing about on my chair, fiddle with my typewriter, and make patterns with the drawing pins on my notice board. Sometimes they are exasperating: like the child who comes to me at 12.00 noon on the last Friday of term when my dinner records have been balanced (in ink) and holds up a fistful of money to me saying, 'I forgot. I'm staying in to dinner today' . . . or the child who sneaks into the office when I am not there and hangs its chlorine-stinking wet swimming things upon my radiator . . . or the child who, looking mournful, comes close to whisper about its sore throat and then coughs in my face. But they can be disarming too: like the child who brings me in a bunch of tulips, obviously stolen from the flower-bed on The Hill; or the child who presents me with a crumpled, grubby, but painstakingly made Christmas card; or the child who creeps up behind me in the playground and slips an affectionate little hand into mine.

And what do the children think of me? I find that this depends upon their age. The children in Mrs Snow's class are very respectful. They know that Mr Masterton is the Most Important Person in the school. As I have an office next to Mr Masterton's they think that I am the Next Most Important Person in the school. They also think I'm rich (because of all that dinner money they bring into the office each day) and a few of them think that I am Mr Masterton's wife. As the children progress through the school they learn that I look after lost property, put plasters upon bleeding knees, remove splinters with a needle, mend shoes with a staple gun, secure falling knickers (or trousers) with safety pins, give out the shampoo for head lice and sharpen broken pencils. It is to me they come if they have a treasured possession they want 'looked after' during the day – and only I can give permission for the telephone to be used. By the time they reach Mr Appleby's class they have worked out the politics of the situation and they are familiar and friendly. (One of our junior girls, accompanied by an elder sister, once greeted me in town on a Saturday morning. 'Is that one of your teachers?' I heard the older girl ask, as they passed by me. 'Oh no,' came the reply, 'that's only the school secretary.')

If I were asked to give an off-the-cuff opinion of the children we are educating at St. Claude's I should probably say that we are turning out a collection of illiterate mini thugs, sex maniacs and drug addicts. I would, of course, be wrong. There is little doubt that most of St. Claude's pupils are well-balanced, healthy, normal, cared-for children. It is just that the normal, average child passes through unnoticed. It's the others I remember. However, it seems that at St. Claude's we do attract more than our fair share of 'the others'. This is probably because we are a Community School, with a 'progressive' image. This is the conclusion I have come to after talking to other school secretaries. (An aside here – just to make you appreciate that school secretaries rarely have opportunities to chat. The only time they speak to each other is when a child leaves one school for another. School Secretary No. 2 will then telephone School Secretary No. 1 and say – 'We have just admitted Charlie and Winnie Bloggs; will you please send on their records.' Each school secretary involved in this conversation will, undoubtedly, have a queue of parents and/or children at their desk, several impatient members of staff hovering, and the knowledge that an overcrowded day is in front of them. There is rarely time to gossip.)

Nevertheless, from talking to my colleagues in other schools I have come to the conclusion that the school secretary who has the easiest time is the one who mans a modern (i.e. built since 1945) primary school in a respectable and long-established working-class council housing estate. In these schools the children usually have parents who are married to each other and are living together. Dad is usually in full-time honest employment and Mum is the good sort of person who considers that being respectable (i.e. paying the bills, cleaning the windows, and keeping a tidy front garden) is of paramount importance. Such parents fork out regularly for dinners, school funds and 'trips' without argument, and turn up dutifully for parents' evenings, Christmas concerts and Sports Days. Children at schools in upper-class areas often have parents who are living apart, au pairs who send them to school inadequately dressed and who fail to turn up to collect them at the end of the day, and mothers who 'never-have-change' to pay for school dinners. Children from lower-class areas have parents who (a) hit the teacher, (b) turn up to collect their offspring whilst staggeringly drunk, (c) break into the school after dark and steal the carpets, or (d) mug the secretary on the way to the post office. Secretaries who man the inner-city inter-racial schools have the most delicate path to tread. The Local Authority will spend extra money upon such schools – and the ratio of numbers of teachers to pupils is a generous one. But the staff are chosen with great political care (any teaching-post applicant who happens to be coloured and Jewish, with one mid-European grandparent, is halfway home) and the eyes of the Press and Radio are upon the school all the time – waiting for something newsworthy to happen.

At St. Claude's, situated between the inner-city ghettos, the upper-class mansions, and the respectable Council flats, we have a fair sprinkling of all three classes of families. But, as a Community School, we also get the drifters.

Now that it is no longer a sin to be unmarried and pregnant there is a growing number of young women with babies, but without husbands. Independent-minded young women with strong anti-marriage convictions usually hold all-embracing anti-Establishment convictions which often include an emphatic distrust of the Education System. Whilst their *minds* might be independent, their day-to-day physical needs are normally met by the Welfare State and/or a boyfriend, and – as other children come along – the family wanders from commune to bed-sitter trying to find an ideal situation in which to live the sort of life they consider to be worthwhile. Sometimes these children go to private 'progressive' schools (where the teachers are often untrained and the curriculum doesn't involve anyone actually *working*) and sometimes, because of frequent changes of address, they avoid educational entanglements altogether. When such children reach the age of 8 or 9 and are still unable to read or write, their parents sometimes begin to have doubts. Perhaps they *should* sample the State System after all. They look around for a suitable school that might not be too damaging to their child's personality. If they are currently in this city, they end up at St. Claude's.

Within our catchment area there are two communes. One has a definitely religious basis. I don't know what the religion is but it involves the children coming to school wearing orange turbans and they seem to eat nothing but nuts and bananas. The children are clean, docile and dim. I have not seen any of the men from this commune, but the women who come to the school wear long dresses and serene smiles; the smiles of people who Know they are Right. The second commune is a gathering of people with artistic leanings. There is at least one minor professional painter amongst them and a few photographers. Occasionally the police raid this commune and take away drugs and pornographic material.

At present we have only one child coming to St. Claude's from this commune. He is a bright lad, but given to having insane rages, when he goes berserk in the playground and attacks other children with an uncontrollable viciousness that takes two dinner ladies to restrain. We have never discovered the reason for these outbursts. We think perhaps the other children taunt him – but he has never said so. Sobbing incoherently, he is eventually led away to recover himself gradually . . . in the office. The children from the communes don't usually stay with us for long. Whether this is because of the parents' renewed disapproval of the State Systrem, or whether it's because of some domestic upheaval in the commune, we never know. One day they are with us – and the next day they are gone; and we might get to hear that they have gone potato picking in Gloucestershire, or are following the pilgrims' path to Canterbury. (A family of six left us last week. They had been travelling the country with a group of gipsies before bringing their head lice and neuroses to St. Claude's; they have now gone off to a self-sufficiency tepee camp in mid Wales.)

Mr Masterton accepts these transient, wayward (and usually unclean) waifs with all the benevolence and magnanimity of a committed teacher (albeit one who rarely enters a classroom, and also spends much time away from school attending Courses, Conferences, Seminars and Study Groups). His secretary is not so magnanimous, and is unashamedly discriminative when prospective families turn up in the office during Mr Masterton's absence.

The Boat People, for example. They turned up one morning at the beginning of last term. At about 9.30 a.m. the office door burst open and this family came in. The man was tall and thoughtful, quiet and worried-looking, with a beard and a crumpled knitted pullover with holes at the elbows. The woman was short, fat and cheerful, with a round, somewhat dirty face, and her clothes hung around her in loops. (I think she was wearing a long skirt *and* trousers, with a shawl over her shoulders, but I can remember only the impression – not the detail.) One hefty boy, of about 10 years, made straight for the radiator and started climbing up it. A female child of about 8 years grabbed the handle of my Banda duplicator and started turning it energetically – backwards. As the parents made no move to control the children I got up from my seat and caught hold of the hand that was enthusiastically ruining my Banda duplicator. Immediately I vacated my seat the third child (female, aged about 6) jumped into it and started whizzing itself round and round. Lifting the whizzing child from my chair I looked up at the adults and said 'Can I help you?' The lately-whizzing child then plunged a hand into my open top drawer and withdrew a fistful of paperclips, elastic bands, two pencils and a staple remover, all of which it threw into the air over its head. 'We've just moved into the area,' the woman explained, 'our house-boat is moored at the docks. We're looking at schools around here to find a suitable place for our children.'

Brushing a few paperclips out of my hair, I resisted the impulse to describe to them a *very* suitable place for their children, and asked them instead exactly where in the docks their house-boat was moored. The location was important. When they told me that they were just beyond the old ferry crossing I beamed with relief. 'Ah, well, that brings you into the Commercial Street School catchment area,' I said. The woman sniffed juicily, wiped her nose on the back of her hand, and said, 'Education's too important to be restricted by political boundaries. I don't want my children's creative instincts to be *cramped* at all; children should be *developed*, and not *hampered*. Don't you agree?' The boy now had his feet planted upon the horizontal pipe running along the floor underneath the radiator, whilst his hands clutched the radiator top. He was making curious knee-bend lunging movements. I wondered just how much 6-stone leverage the old cast iron radiator would stand, and said that I agreed absolutely and that I thought she might find St. Claude's a little formal. 'We chant tables here,' I said darkly, 'and the children have to march in silence to a religious assembly each day,' I lied. The woman looked shocked. '*Do* go and have a look at Commercial Street School,' I urged, 'I'm sure you won't find any *hampering* there.' There was a sudden CRASH from Mr Masterton's office. The youngest child had found its way in there and had pulled over the gobe atlas.

Between us the woman and I rounded up the children and I ushered them out of the office – and I gave them precise directions on how to get to Commercial Street School. During all this time the man had neither said nor done anything. He just stood there, looking miserably thoughtful. He now followed us out of the school and trailed behind his family down the street. In my last glimpse of them I saw the boy grab hold of the radio aerial protruding from Mrs Snow's car and snap it off. I quickly withdrew into the school and sent up a prayer to our patron saint. '*Please*, St. Claude; deliver us from the Boat People.' St. Claude must have heard and taken notice. We have not seen the Boat People since.

St. Claude's is like a kaleidoscope. Each term the kaleidoscope is shaken, and the pattern changes. Some children come – and others go; and all I remember is a solemn little face beneath a knitted bobble cap; a chest-tearing cough heard in the corridor; five perfectly-formed but filthy toes hanging out from a tattered plimsoll; tears of distress on plump cheeks, or hearty glee-filled laughter from a mouth filled with decayed teeth. These children are the innocent fragments of a torn society. I book their names into the St. Claude's School Admittance Register. And a few months later I book them out again.

But there is a certain hard-core of stability in the St. Claude's kaleidoscope. Some children have spent all their school lives with us, and some of them are the children of parents who also spent their school lives at St. Claude's. The Hulbert brothers are a good example. Ricky Hulbert is in Mr Singleton's class, and his brother Darren is with Miss Krantz. Their sister Tina will be starting with Mrs Snow next term, and the last time I saw Mrs Hulbert (the title is a courtesy one; so far as we are aware there has never been a *Mr* Hulbert) she was heavily pregnant and there will no doubt be another little Hulbert joining us in $4\frac{1}{2}$ year's time. Mrs Hulbert (who is in her late 20s) can remember being in Mr Singleton's class when she attended St. Claude's, and she lives with her mother (known as Old Gran Hulbert) who also attended the school back in the 1930s and who has been producing healthy Hulbert offspring since the 1940s. Most of her children live in the area, and there is another young Hulbert (Sandra – aged about 13) who actually shares the flat with Old Gran and young Mrs Hulbert, and we aren't sure which of the Hulbert women is her mother. Sandra Hulbert is now at secondary school. She wears skin-tight denim trousers, high heels, earrings, black-rimmed eyes and pink spiky hair. Each time I have seen her she has been ambling along the main road surrounded and followed by a small crowd of similarly dressed and grinning youths, and I've no doubt that Sandra is going to maintain the Hulbert family tradition of enthusiastic fecundity.

But, returning to the Hulbert brothers who are currently attending St. Claude's school . . . they are naughty. They are extremely naughty. They lie, steal, fight, swear, play truant and generally vandalise with a persistence that has even Mr Singleton almost admitting defeat. But they are well fed, cheerful and happy; they have the emotional support of a large and loving family, and the stabilising influence of the many Hulbert uncles and great uncles living in the area, most of whom encourage the children in the traditional Hulbert pursuits of lying, stealing, fighting, vandalising and avoiding employment. I am convinced that beating the children would be as useless (almost) as attempting to reason with them. So we all just try and cope with them on a day to day basis, accepting that if windows are broken, dinner money stolen, toilet rolls pushed down lavatory pans, obscene words chalked up in the corridor – the Hulbert brothers will be in some way involved, but that actually proving it, or doing anything to stop it happening again is probably not possible.

Ricky has an engaging smile (which wins large second helpings of pudding from Mrs Beagle) and his playground violence is, admittedly, usually provoked by the need to go to the defence of his younger brother who is slightly deaf, a little bit stupid, and is often picked on by other children. But Ricky's most interesting talent is his ability to talk, at length, around a situation. His explanation for stealing another boy's watch would go something like this. 'Well, we was in the toilet and this kid had a watch and Marcus said I'll swap you with something, and then this other kid, not the one with the watch, said all right and then Paul came in and then we went into the corridor and there was a bit of a fight, I don't know who started it but this other kid. No, I mean. Well, you see this kid said my brother was stupid and so I pushed him and then someone said Mr Singleton's coming so we went into the classroom. And then we were all talking and I accidentally put the watch in my pocket.' Ricky has given similar long-winded explanations for 'accidentally' kicking another boy in the face, throwing a chair through the dining-room window, pushing a girl's jacket down the lavatory pan, and stealing the coach driver's lunch box. Mr Singleton is the only member of staff who has, so far, managed to keep Ricky sitting quietly at his desk during lesson times, but even he has failed to get the boy to do any work. One success that Mr Singleton has scored is in cutting down on the amount of truanting. Mr Singleton doesn't allow truanting. Mr Singleton puts on his trilby hat and overcoat and, summoning Mr Masterton to keep an eye on his class, he goes in pursuit. And having coped with two generations of truanting Hulberts, he knows just where to look. (The last time Mr Singleton went on a truant hunt in the old dockside warehouses he came back with Ricky in tow, and two of Mr Appleby's boys who hadn't been missed.)

In a couple of years' time Ricky will have moved on to secondary education, and the other two Hulberts will be 'working' their way through the school. So, although the

St. Claude's Admittance Register would, on a casual inspection, suggest a large turnover of children, the repetition of the name Hulbert gives a reassuring sense of permanence.

Another child who has been with us all his school life is Jason Spragg. Jason is now in his last year, with Mr Appleby, and I have watched him progress class by class through the school. I can remember him in Mrs Snow's class – an angelic-looking little boy with a shock of golden/white curly hair around a face of exquisitely cherubic proportions and large trusting blue eyes. I can remember going into Mrs Snow's class on one occasion and seeing Jason sitting at a diminutive table alongside a little girl who was very seriously drawing a large sun on a piece of paper. Her left arm, plumply rounded, lay across her piece of paper. Jason picked up his pencil and looked at the point. He then deliberately, and with all his force, plunged the pencil point into the soft round arm beside him. The little girl screamed and jumped up clutching her arm. Her chair fell onto the floor behind her and Mrs Snow appeared from the book corner to see what was happening. Jason immediately burst into tears and rushed towards Mrs Snow crying 'She kicked me; she kicked me!' and he buried his little golden head in her skirt.

I can remember another occasion when Jason was in Miss Krantz's class. I was watching from the staffroom window as the children were playing 'Statues' in the playground. In case you have forgotten how to play Statues I will remind you that the children line up and the person 'on it' takes each child's hand in turn and swings the child out into the playground. The child has to stagger into a certain position and then maintain it without moving. When the line of children has been thus transformed into 'statues' the person 'on it' goes around and inspects each one carefully. The first child to wobble or fall over has lost that round of the game, and is therefore 'on it' . . . and the rest of the children line up again. I noticed, from my staffroom observation point, that each time Jason was 'on it' the children seemed to be flung into the playground with unnecessary force. I also noticed that each time Jason was 'on it' he moved nearer and nearer to the climbing frame. Fortunately Mr Scott, who was on playground duty, got there just in time to catch a child who was being flung, face first, into the steel upright of the Giant Rocket.

Jason is an intelligent boy, and very well-behaved in class. His work is neat, tidy and above average, and he always volunteers to help his teacher when it comes to giving out pencils or clearing up at the end of the lesson. Miss Krantz found him useful because he never minded washing out the paintpots at the end of the afternoon, and Mr Scott was delighted when Jason offered to clean his car in the lunch break. When he moved into Mr Singleton's class Jason decided to take up cello lessons, and Mr Singleton considered that the boy had 'promise'. It wasn't until Jason reached Mr Appleby's class that concern was felt for his behaviour. It was Mrs Barron, the playground lady, who first put it into words. 'He's a bloody sadist that kid!' she said, hauling Jason into the office one lunchtime. Jason, by this time tall, blonde and with an elegant swagger, had collected a band of cronies who followed him everywhere. Jason and his cronies had, apparently, singled out a particularly sensitive junior girl and had cornered the child during the lunchtime to announce 'Your mother is dead; we know because the school has just received a message from the hospital to say she was knocked down by a lorry.' Jason had to spend his lunchtime during the next fortnight sitting in the office writing out the lines 'I must not tell lies', but within two weeks of being allowed out again he was being marched back in by Mrs Barron.

This time Jason and his band of followers had invaded the infant playground during the lunch break and, selecting an infant girl who was by herself in a corner of the playground, had surrounded her and just stood there silently staring at her – moving closer and closer – until the child, in a state of knicker-wetting terror, had screeched for assistance. 'But we didn't *do* anything,' protested Jason, with an air of offended dignity. 'We didn't say a *thing*'. Other incidents were noticed. When Mr Appleby's class were filing down the corridor to Assembly, the child walking in front of Jason always seemed to fall down the corridor steps. When St. Claude's were playing football against a neighbouring school, Jason's opponent always seemed to suffer some sort of unfortunate injury. During morning and afternoon playtimes when the playground was supervised by a teacher, there were few problems with Jason and, for a long time, Jason's lunchtime behaviour (including 'accidental' kicking of the playground ladies) was not taken seriously by Mr Masterton. 'The boy just needs careful handling,' he explained to me one day, 'Our playground ladies *mean* well, of course, but they haven't been *trained* to control and guide children.'

But then the occasion came when Mr Masterton, chancing to cross the playground one dinnertime, saw Jason pin a small Chinese boy against a wall. Yanking the child's head back by his hair, Jason spat full into his face. Mr Masterton was appalled. He marched Jason up to the office and made him stand outside in the corridor with his face to the wall. 'I think it would be a good idea to send for his parents,' he said to me. I too thought it would be a good idea; but didn't think it would be possible. I had tried contacting one of the Spraggs on previous occasions regarding non-payment of dinner money, but could never get hold of them. Mr Spragg, a solicitor, was always 'in Court' or 'with a Client', and his wife Dr Evelyn Spragg, a lecturer at the Polytechnic, was equally unobtainable. (The Polytechnic is a large place, with short-tempered telephonists, and Dr Spragg didn't believe in keeping the school informed of her various extension numbers.)

However, face-spitting being of more concern than dinner-money collecting, I made a determined effort on this occasion, and actually insisted that Dr Spragg be summoned to the telephone from the Lecture Hall. She was furious. 'Good God above; you can't expect me to become involved in settling every trivial playground fight! Surely Mr Masterton doesn't need me to tell him how to control the children in his care!' She refused to come. So Mr Masterton took the only course of action left open to him. He imposed a lunchtime ban on Jason for the next fortnight. He wrote to Mr and Dr Spragg and asked them to make arrangements for Jason's care and supervision each day between 12.00 noon and 1.30 p.m. until the end of the month. This may not have been much of a punishment for Jason . . . but it most certainly was for his parents.

The one child in his class whom Jason never taunts is May Watts. May is a thin and dirty ten-year-old child who

76

has been with us for almost a year now. May has hair that is long, shaggy and 'suspect', and legs that are bony and scarred with scratched and bleeding flea-bites. She has clear blue eyes that are hidden behind grimy glasses, and there is usually a cold sore lurking somewhere between nose and mouth. May has two ferret-like younger twin sisters whom she drags up the hill each day and upon whom she lavishes mother-like bossy affection. When the trio reaches the playground May will fuss around the twins making sure they are fit for presentation to Miss Krantz. With grubby fingers she pushes and primps at their hair; going down on one knee she will tug at a filthy cardigan and carefully fasten the one remaining button. With a smoothing of each skirt, and a careful folding-down of each muddy sock top, she will then push the two little girls into Miss Krantz's classroom before racing off to join Mr Appleby's class.

May Watts is ferocious in defence of her sisters and herself. Although much lighter in weight than anyone else in her class she will take on any playground challenger by wading in with flying fists and feet. (I can remember, one dinner hour, hastily looking aside and passing on my way when I saw May's fist land, with power born of fury, upon Jason's trouser zip. When I glanced back Jason was staggering about the playround bent double. For a moment I reflected with concern about the possible consequences awaiting May after school – but then brushed these worries aside. I had seen May, in a temper, after school. With one twin clutched in either hand she took her stand on the pavement – defiance and anger glaring out from her smeary glasses. May, even handicapped with glasses and the twins, was a match for Jason Spragg.)

But May isn't by nature aggressive; she is pathetically eager to please. She dances into the office each playtime and dinnertime asking if she can *do* anything. As she doesn't smell very nice, and I don't want her hanging about the office, I usually give her the dinner registers to take back to the classrooms, or send her with a message to one of the teachers. But sometimes I can think of no reason to send her away; so she stands beside me and chats about her mum, her dad, the twins and her baby brother. Mum and dad don't get up very early, I gather, and so May gets the twins ready for school and gives the baby his bottle. When she gets home from school, Dad's not there, but Mum is, and so May gets the tea, and when Dad comes home she goes across to the chip shop and gets their supper. Mum isn't very well, May tells me, and so she needs looking after. May's mother didn't look very well when I first saw her about eleven months ago when she registered the children for admission to St. Claude's. She was a fat, complaining woman, totally unable to cope with the vagaries of life thrust upon her by being obliged to follow her labouring husband who worked upon motorway contracts that took him up and down the British Isles. But now they were settled. Dad had got a job with the Gas Board. 'He's working in a trench down Commercial Street,' May told me proudly.

Another child whose behaviour ensures that she will always be remembered by the St. Claude's staff is Marlene Coggins. Marlene is a pretty child with long fair hair, a pale face and 'interesting' grey-blue eyes. She is affectionate, generous, has a sunny nature, and was one of Mrs Snow's favourites when Marlene was in her class. The only faults showing at this stage were those of bossiness, and a desire to be the centre of attraction, but as this meant that Marlene could be relied upon to perform with charm and enthusiasm in Mrs Snow's concerts, she was forgiven. Marlene – graceful and uninhibited when dancing or singing – was often to be seen in the playground bossily organising other children into taking part in little fantasies that she had created (and which gave her a leading role) but when one playtime Miss Krantz found a group of infants playing Doctors and Nurses behind a cupboard in her room, we got the first hint of the troubles that lay ahead. Doctors and Nurses meant everyone taking off their knickers and trousers and taking it in turns to explore each other with a pencil.

In the happy-go-lucky atmosphere of Mr Scott's class Marlene always chose to do her work on the floor – kneeling with her elbows on the mat and her frilly backside in the air. As Marlene was, at that time, a diligent, if slow, worker Mr Scott didn't object to this, until the day he discovered that Marlene was distracting the rest of the class by assuming the same posture without her knickers on. Mrs Coggins was sent for and she promised that in future she would check each day that Marlene came to school properly dressed. When Mrs Coggins walked into the office I knew I was looking at Marlene in twenty years' time. Mrs Coggins – pretty, with long fair hair, a pale face and 'interesting' grey-blue eyes – walked with a suggestive movement of the hips and she grasped Mr Masterton's arm with an affectionate and clinging gesture. 'I'm *dreadfully* worried about Marlene,' she said, gazing up. at him intently. Mr Masterton ushered her hastily into his office . . . and left the door wide open.

As Marlene moved up the school her bossiness and dramatic displays became more of a nuisance. In Mr Singleton's class she was obliged to sit tidily at her desk during lesson time, but certain out-of-class incidents stick out in my mind; like the playtime when Marlene – on top of the climbing frame with her legs spread wide apart – screeched dramatically that she was 'stuck' and attracted a group of upward-glancing giggling boys beneath her, and it was found that once again she had 'forgotten' her knickers. Then there was the affair of the handsome Italian YOB student who had to be hastily returned to base after it was discovered that he was meeting Marlene after school. But it is undoubtedly the attention Marlene pays to the visiting workmen that causes Mr Masterton most worry. Marlene is now a sylph-like ten-year-old in Mr Appleby's class, and any man coming into the school wearing overalls and carrying a ladder, screwdriver or paintpot is liable, upon pausing in his work, to find Marlene, smelling of 'Intimate Passion' perfume, snuggling against his trouser legs and stroking his hand with soft red-tipped fingers.

Marlene's mother runs a Sauna. Situated in the main road between The Bunch of Grapes and the fish shop, Marlene's mother specialises in providing massage, hair removal, steam baths, beauty therapy and general relaxation in the perfumed steamy waters of her Jacuzzi spa whirlpool bath. From time to time Mr Masterton sends a letter home asking Mrs Coggins to see that Marlene doesn't come to school wearing make-up and perfume – and he always receives a prompt reply. Mrs Coggins, writing in a large flowing hand, replies upon jumbo-sized pink paper to the effect that she does *try* to make Marlene be discreet in her make-up but as the child loves helping out in the Sauna it is very difficult to keep her away from the perfume . 'And Marlene is *so* interested in the beauty business' she wrote in her last letter 'and *so* anxious to make the best of herself.' (This letter came reeking of 'Wild Allure' which certainly, for a few hours, made the office smell better than it usually does.)

It seems that Marlene's interests are exclusively in the 'beauty business' because she has fallen behind academically as she has progressed through the school; moreover – to Mr Singleton's exasperation – she shows no real interest in music in spite of possessing a remarkably powerful bell-like soprano voice and a sense of rhythm, emotional expression and dramatic performance which makes her a star in every school musical production. Certainly Marlene loves acting, but I get the impression that she would prefer to do her own song and dance act without any direction from Mr Singleton. And there are always rows about what she wears. Mr Singleton likes his choir to appear neatly dressed in grey skirts (or trousers) and clean white blouses (or shirts) and the nearest Mrs Coggins ever got to providing such garments was a drooping grey dirndl skirt and a rather revealing frilly blouse that Marlene wore one Christmas.

But last Easter Marlene made no effort to conform. She turned up at the Easter Concert wearing some high-heeled sling-back shoes of her mother's, red fish-net long socks, a very short red skirt and a skin-tight white T shirt. She was also wearing make-up and had painted her fingernails dark blue. The Occasion was a special Singleton-arrangement of parts of the Messiah for recorders and junior voices – and Mr Singleton was furious. He made Marlene wash her face and remove her shoes and fish-net socks in the classroom. Marlene padded around in her bare feet, pouting and looking sulky and saying she wasn't going to sing then. As the highlight of the performance was to be an aria by Marlene I wondered which way the Coggins love of drama was going to exhibit itself; to sing – and be noticed; not to sing – and create a dramatic silence.

As things turned out Marlene rose to the occasion nobly. After a spirited Singleton-adapation of 'Oh Thou that

Bringest Good Tidings' by the recorders, the orchestra rearranged itself for the solo. The choir were sitting cross-legged on the floor, with Marlene amongst them. Under Mr Singleton's gently waving hands the strings eased their way into a short introduction – and Marlene stood up. Clasping one hand of murky fingernails into the other, she took a deep breath and sang . . . 'I *know* that-at my Redeemer Liveth'. She hit that top note with pure, unwavering, accuracy, and she sang with the ecstasy of a sinner in Paradise. We were all enraptured. The audience in the hall stared up in wonderment at the slight red-skirted figure with the voice of such sweetness. The children in the front row of the choir turned round from their positions on the floor and stared up at her; the boys sitting on the floor either side of her stared up at her . . . and the irreverent thought went through my mind that, once again, Marlene had probably forgotten her knickers.

There are 22 children at St. Claude's who would, in common parlance, be classed as 'coloured' – which is a foolish expression because in fact there is not a face in the school (with the possible expection of Marlene's, when it's washed) that is actually white. The 22 children I am referring to have Oriental, Mediterranean or African origins and they range in colour from the yellowy-white of our two Chinese families, through the olive-white of our Turkish and Indian families to the brown and glossy-black of the children whose ancestors were African. We have several coal-black children in the top two classes and a sprinkling of mid-brown faces throughout each class in the school. Seven of our black children live with middle-class 'white' parents who adopted them when they were babies and although mostly they appear to be well-balanced children (who speak with middle-class accents) two of them are moody and aggressive, and I wonder if their adoptive parents are now regretting the philanthropic gesture they felt they made to society eight or nine years ago. Of the other black/brown children in the school, four are from families that moved in recently from the Caribbean, two are from a mixed marriage, and three are the result of mixed mistakes made by a cheerful girl who has children of various shades of brown in three classes at St. Claude's.

There appears to be complete racial harmony amongst the children in the infants' classes, yet I sense a rather over-protective attitude by teaching and playground staff towards those children whose skins have tones of brown. (I have noticed that whereas terms of abuse like 'Dirty Jew', 'Irish Dope', or 'Yellow-faced Chink' are dismissed as normal playground vernacular, any whisper of 'Blackie' or 'Nig-Nog' causes great consternation.) Last week, for example, there was a fracas in the infants' playground when Leroy (5 years – black face – black curls) kicked Garry ($4\frac{1}{2}$ years – pink face – golden curls) and called him 'Shit Pants'. Garry (pink face turning to red) pushed Leroy down and called him a 'Dirty Black Bastard'. Miss Krantz, who was on playground duty, marched them both in to the office to account for themselves to Mr Masterton. Leroy and Garry stood side by side in Mr Masteron's office. The door was open and I could hear the cross-examination proceeding. Whereas apparently both boys were 'very naughty', it seems that Garry's crime was the greater. 'That was most unkind,' Mr Masterton said gravely, 'and a very unpleasant thing to say. Why did you behave like this?' Garry wasn't able to offer any acceptable explanation, but it occurred to me that he probably considered one push was equal to one kick – and he had, by now, probably forgotten what they'd both been yelling. But Mr Masterton felt he couldn't leave it there. He blundered on. 'Just because his skin is black and yours is pink, it doesn't mean it's really any different you know.' There was a long pause. Both children remained silent. *'He can't help being black,'* said Mr Masterton finally . . . *'It's not his fault.'* The boys were eventually dismissed – and trotted out from the office with expressionless faces.

On another occasion, when Jason Spragg pulled down the knickers of an Indian girl in his class, I can remember Mr Masterton and Mr Appleby having an earnest discussion trying to decide whether the attack was sexist or racist.

Although there is no obvious racial disharmony in the junior classes, I notice a certain polarisation amongst the children, in that those with brown or black faces play with each other more than with children with white or off-white faces. And, occasionally, there are quarrels.

In Mr Appleby's class there is an energetic, wiry little boy called Georgie. Georgie is the fastest player on the football field and a skilled gymnast. He is cheerful, normally very good-tempered, and has a very black skin. Last summer I accompanied Mr Appleby's class on their outing to the Zoo, and we were all walking along a path that lay between the lake and the caged anthropoids when Emily (tall, with freckles and ginger plaits) pointed to a small monkey swinging from a trapeze in its cage. 'Oh look!' she shrieked, 'there's Georgie!' The whole class stopped, looked, and the children all shouted with laughter. All except Georgie. Georgie dashed forward with fury contorting his little black face. He seized Emily by one arm and flung her into the lake. Emily went headlong into the water and then emerged spluttering and covered with pond weed and water lilies. The class, who had not seen such entertainment for a long time, fell about all over the path howling with renewed laughter whilst Mr Appleby and I pulled Emily from the lake. A young Argentinian, Felipe, clapped Georgie on the back (he never did like Emily), and Georgie grinned. Mr Appleby and I said all the appropriate things, and Mr Appleby proceeded with the class whilst I took the dripping Emily back to school. As a result of this episode I think that lessons have been learned. Emily has learned to keep her opinions to herself, and Georgie has learned that, by force, defeat can be turned into triumph. I am not sure that either lesson will improve black/white relationships within the top class of St. Claude's.

There are no poor children at St. Claude's. Even the dirtiest, most poorly-clad and most undernourished of them come to school wearing quartz digital watches (which they treat with careless indifference) and many have radio-cassette players and video recorders given to them as presents. Practically all of them have roller boots. Roller-skating is the current craze. By the time this is published no doubt roller-skating will be out of fashion and those shoddy but deceptively sturdy-looking plastic boot/skates that now zoom around the playground will have been chucked out, or will lie abandoned in the back of toy cupboards. (Crazes lasted longer when I was a child. I remember owning just *one* leather-strapped steel and ballbearinged roller skate upon which I scuffed around in one-legged enthusiasm for many summers. My skate was stamped with a number and the words 'Pat Pending'. I didn't know who Pat Pending was, or how it came about that she had lost one roller skate. In an unthinking moment I worked out that she could be a one-legged cripple and needed only one skate, but I never really believed this foolish notion. So I scuffed along the streets a little anxiously, half-expecting Pat Pending to rush out from a doorway and claim back her skate.)

But although we have no poor children at St. Claude's, there are quite a few neglected ones; children who are sent to school without any breakfast or who have no-one to go home to in the afternoon; children who are never taken for their appointments at the dental hospital or eye clinic; and children who are sent to school when they are ill. I have noticed that many of our mothers who are in employment (whether they are secretaries, sociologists or shop assistants) turn a blind eye and a deaf ear to their child's streaming eyes, high temperature and hacking cough. If the child can actually stand it's shoved inside the school door – and mother makes a quick getaway.

About two-thirds of our children – whatever the colour of their skin or their social background – have a common predicament, i.e. an irregular home life. Just under half of the children come from single-parent homes and, of the remaining children, I know that a large number of them go home to parents one of whom is really an itinerant 'Uncle' or 'Aunt' or 'friend'. Of the 160 children at St. Claude's only about 40 of them go home to mothers who are waiting for them with the tea laid, and legitimate fathers who will come home later from work. No wonder that, when sending letters home from school, I daren't address the envelope 'Mr & Mrs Brown', or Mr & Mrs Jenkins'. I cannot be expected to remember whether Tom Brown or Mary Jenkins *has* a mother or father currently at home or, if they have, what name they are using. Every letter to a parent sent out from St. Claude's School, therefore, is addressed to 'The parent of . . .' I know that of the letters that are sent home about one-third will be torn apart and used as paper darts before the end of the road; a third will simply get 'lost' and the remaining third will, albeit crumpled and torn, end up in the hand of the parent. When giving out letters I try to stress the importance of their content, whilst assuring the child that there is nothing to worry about. But I can't say 'Take this home and give it to Mummy or Daddy,' so I phrase my advice to suit the circumstances. 'It's about the school concert (camp/ jumble sale/sports day/dinner money),' I say. 'Make sure you look after it . . . and *give it to someone at home*.'

CHAPTER SIX

Dirt and Dinners

Whilst sorting out the dinner registers the other day I saw a flea hopping across my desk. I dithered for a few seconds – not knowing whether to thump it with my hand, or try and make a more skilful attack with a ruler . . . and then it disappeared. It was, unfortunately, hopping towards me at the time of its disappearance. I mentioned this to Mr Potts and he said that Mrs Penfold the cleaner had been complaining recently about the fleas in the school – alleging that one had, in fact, jumped up inside her trouser leg. 'I reckon it's that last lot of jumble we had in,' Mr Potts said, 'there was a right grotty fur coat amongst it.'

Fleas, head lice, malodorous children, and corridors smelling faintly of lavatories and wet clothes are accepted as normal conditions of life at St. Claude's, along with the dirty windows, battered doors and grubby finger-marked walls. With 160 children invading the place each day – and only Mr & Mrs Potts and Mrs Penfold to clean up behind them – this is, perhaps, not surprising. Neither is it surprising that Mrs Penfold is always grumbling and threatening to leave. At the start of each term we come into a school that has clean-scrubbed walls, shining desks and floors, and corridors that smell sweetly of polish. Within two days we are back to normal, and an exasperated Mrs Penfold is chasing children with her broom and a patient Mrs Potts is mopping up in the children's lavatories and trying to obliterate noisome smells with disinfectant.

The rest of us don't help very much either. Having come

to accept these conditions as 'normal' we wear our scruffiest clothes to school, shrug our shoulders at spilt paint, glue, milk and blood, and are careless and unthinking when it comes to cleaning the tools and equipment we handle daily. Our staffroom coffee mugs are a good example and I am beginning to think that we must all have dual standards of cleanliness. I would guess that each one of us would insist upon clean cutlery and cups at home, and yet we cheerfully pig it in the staffroom with most unwholesome-looking crockery. The only person who tries to clean things up a bit is Mrs Potts who brews the morning coffee. She supplies us with dishcloths and washing-up liquid, and she keeps the milk saucepan clean. But when the bell goes for the end of playtime, each morning and afternoon, most members of staff make a dash for the sink, give their cups a perfunctory swill and dump them on the draining board. Nobody puts anything away or wipes down the draining board or washes the teapot or cleans out the washing-up bowl. (Mr Singleton, who brings his coffee in a thermos flask, has never been seen within a yard of the staffroom sink.)

When I first came to work in a school I was slightly taken aback by the general scruffiness of the staffroom. But I soon adjusted, and eventually became fond of the homely atmosphere. I came to like the clutter of footballs, old fish tanks and broken guitars in the corners; the toppling piles of magazines and papers on the table. I got used to stepping around people who were cutting out large sheets of paper on the floor, and I came to enjoy sinking into an armchair, even though the springs were broken and the fabric grimy. After a while I didn't notice the threadbare mats, the cracked and scuffed skirting boards and the dark area of dirt on the floor around each immovable object (like the lockers, cupboards and sink unit). I only find it embarrassing when we get visitors from outside the education system who don't understand how things are.

An opportunity for seeing ourselves as others see us came last year when a playground lady who was leaving asked if she could take a photograph of all the staff. Those of us who could be rounded up stood against the playground wall and smiled dutifully into her camera. She came back a few weeks later and pinned up a copy on the staffroom notice board – with a little note to say we could each order one for 20p. I gazed at it in astonishment. Did my hair really stick out like that? And surely, my shoes weren't really so down-at-heel as they appeared? That pullover! It's a very good quality one; why does it look so droopy? The other members of staff looked equally scruffy. Mr Singleton, his trousers bagging at the knees and his sports jacket bulging at the pockets; Mr Appleby – a middle-aged hippy in tight jeans and a roll-necked sweater. Mr Masterton, his face a little blurred above his neatly pointed beard, stood tall and stooping, looking like a dignified, if rather weary, goat; and Miss Krantz, blank-faced behind her glasses, was wearing a blouse that bulged lumpily at every button. Even Mrs Snow, who normally wears very expensive and classy clothes, looked somewhat battered in a skirt with a drooping hemline and which was splodged in powder paint. The photograph stayed on the notice board until it curled at the edges and someone threw it away. I don't think anyone ordered a copy.

One small area of the school which Mrs Potts manages to keep clean and presentable is the staff toilet – even though her task is made difficult by the large number of people other than staff who nip in there during the course of the day. Visitors, Mrs Potts accepts, are bona fide users of the staff toilet and also, on occasions, mothers who have come to help. But she gets rather upset about the casual use of the place by mothers who are delivering or collecting their children, or workmen (who always leave the seat up) meter readers, delivery men, or anyone else passing in the street who has been 'taken short'. (Declaring 'This is not a public toilet' I have known her bar the way to someone she found hastening in from outside . . . only to finally relent and allow access 'Just this once mind!') Considering also that many members of staff grope their way into the toilet with hands dirty with paint or ink, I think that Mrs Potts does a sterling job – particularly as she also has to cope with the towel problem.

The cloth hand-towels provided for general use by staff and pupils are contained inside machines. These machines are attached to the wall alongside each sink, or line of sinks. The Local Authority pays the termly bill of a laundry contractor whose job it is to attend the school weekly and change the towels in all machines. But the towel people are a confounded nuisance; they are always letting us down. Moreover, when they do turn up, they frequently replace our limp, sodden and mucky towels with dry and crisply-laundered but equally mucky towels – still covered with the paint and clay daubs of a previous school. Complaining, we have found, is useless. 'No good going on at me,' the man said to Mrs Potts when he last called, 'I only deliver the bloody things.' My telephoned complaint to the Head Office was equally unsuccessful. 'The trouble with you schools', I was told, 'is that you get the towels so damn dirty!'

In the old days we had no trouble with towels. Each member of staff had his/her own personal hand-towel which they took home to wash every Friday and brought back every Monday morning. We each had our own hook in the staff cloakroom. The children used long roller towels. There were two of these alongside the juniors' wash hand basins and two near the infants'. Each Wednesday and Friday they were taken down and replaced by clean ones, and during the following week the school cook washed the children's roller towels along with the kitchen tea towels. The system used to work without any problem that I can recall. But now we have towels in machines . . . and the problems (like the dirty towels) are unending.

To begin with they are awkward to use. The Health and Safety Regulations say that the towel machine must be situated in an elevated position above the sink (so that when you reach up for it, having washed your hands, the water runs down your arms), and there must be no more than a couple of feet of looped towel available at any one pull. From the 18″ of usable towel available I am just about able to dry my small thin hands, and I've no doubt the other ladies can cope equally well. But how Mr Appleby manages with those great podgy fists after a session at the metalwork or pottery class, I can't imagine. (His presumed eagerness to obtain a longer length of dry towel probably accounts for the fact that the machine in the staff cloakroom has been half-yanked off its wall fixing on several occasions.) But the real nuisance arises when we have reached the end of the machine towel and its last three feet hang filthy and limp from the machine . . . and Mrs Potts informs us that 'They haven't turned up again this week.' The children (who have grown up with a system that provides a machine towel that is jammed in the works part of the time, and wet and dirty most of the time) very rarely wash their hands.

Bearing in mind the amount of food which is dropped (and thrown) around the playground, corridors, classrooms and dining hall each playtime and dinner time, it is not surprising that St. Claude's houses and nourishes many families of mice. They are with us all the time. During the normal uproar of a school day you don't often see or hear them but sometimes on a quiet summer's afternoon when the noisiest children are away at games, or during early morning when the whole school is in the Assembly Hall, I can hear them scratching about behind the office cupboards, or bounding across the ceiling rafters. We think there are several families of them living behind the skirting boards of Mrs Snow's classroom (where they feed handsomely upon the stores of gerbil food and also, occasionally, the contents of the bean bags) and we know there is at least one long-tailed field mouse who takes up winter quarters each year underneath the sink unit in the staffroom. Occasionally when Mr Potts thinks a population explosion has occurred amongst our resident mice, he calls in The Authority's Pest Control Officer.

We have found that The Authority's pest control system works quite efficiently when dealing with a complaint of too many mice. A man in a starched white coat attends the school within a few days of Mr Potts' telephone call, and little plastic dishes of poison are laid in discreet places behind cupboards in every room. By the end of the week a vague stink, rather nastier than normal, creeps through the corridors and rooms, and within a month Mr Potts is able to report that 'There are less of them about now'. But trying to get rid of rats is a different matter. For some bureaucratic reason The Authority calls in an outside contractor to deal with rats; but we can never be sure which outside contractor currently has The Authority's Rat Catching Contract. The system is that each school must ring The Authority to find out this information. On the last occasion I had to seek it I was given only a telephone number – and the rat catcher in question seemed to have his telephone connected permanently to an answering machine. Three weeks went by before anyone actually came.

Whilst most of us tolerate a few mice around the school – (after all, unlike fleas and head lice, one isn't in danger of becoming personally involved with them) – rats are different. The sight of a thick grey shape loping across the dining-room floor one evening had Mrs Penfold rushing straight out of school to catch her bus home, and even our toughie junior boys came pell mell into the office one afternoon to report in horror that an evil pointed face was looking up at them from the playground drain. Mrs Beagle, the cook, who sets and empties mousetraps in the kitchen as a matter of daily routine, who removes cockroaches by the handful from the back of her cupboards, and who will argue the toss with delivery men or Local Authority Catering Supervisors without flinching, is terrified of rats. One morning when she found some rat droppings on the floor of her kitchen she refused to start the job of dinner preparation until Mr Masterton had personally opened all her cupboard doors to ascertain that no rat lurked inside.

Trying to get hold of the Rat Man on that particular occasion produced a new set of difficulties. Having got through to the appropriate department of The Authority (in itself an achievement as the extension was engaged for about twenty minutes) I dialled the number I was given and the telephone was promptly answered by a crisp female voice. I probably got off to a bad start by humorously asking if that was the Pied Piper, and then when I carried on to explain our problem I was told to 'Put it on a 492AS.' From then on the conversation went something like this: Me: 'Pardon?' Female voice (louder and clearer): 'A 492AS.' Me (still trying to be humorous): 'Until it's caught it can't be put on anything, and I don't think a 492AS would be big enough anyway.' There was a long silent pause whilst this witticism was digested. Me: 'Hello.' Female voice: 'Yes?' Me: 'What about this rat?' Female voice: 'As I said, you'll have to put it on a 492AS.' Further attempts at humour being abandoned I asked for an explanation and was told that a 492AS was an Official Authority Small Order Form, of which I had never heard, and without which the Rat Catching Company was prepared to do nothing. 'If you could just quote me an order number it would help,' said the Female Voice. 'Will *any* order number do?' I asked, immediately seeing a loophole. 'Oh no; it must be a 492AS,' she said. I told her I would ring her back. When I next saw Mr Potts, about an hour later, I asked him, 'What have you done with the 492AS's?' He said 'Pardon?'

Mr Potts is an enterprising man. Shortly after this conversation he returned to the office carrying a small order pad, yellowing and curling at the edges, with the heading EDUCATION BOARD REQUISITIONS at the top. The place to indicate the date was indicated thus: .... 194... and the order pad number had reached 280 – in front of which Mr Potts had seen fit to write in biro 000. In the opposite corner of the pad Mr Potts had marked in bold biro '492AS'. He asked if I thought this would do and I said I was sure it would. I rang the Rat Catcher and the Female Voice accepted without question our Order No. 000280, and promised to send someone along immediately. I told her that when their man called he could collect the order form – upon which I had typed: 'Please attend to problem of rats in school'. Mr Masterton looked slightly puzzled as he signed it. 'Funny . . . I don't remember seeing these forms before'.

Fortunately I don't have to send for the Rat Catcher very often. I don't think this is because we have so few rats – (some of those feet that go pounding across my ceiling seem a bit too heavy-footed for mere mice) – but because most of our rats are discreet and rarely put in an appearance, and Mrs Beagle would be the first to admit that rats, mice and cockroaches are the least of her problems.

Mrs Beagle's kitchen is a large room at the end of the school, with quarry-tiled floor, fitted cupboards with 'easiclene' wipeover surfaces and a high sloping ceiling that suffers from permanent damp (because of roofleaks plus steam) and which drops white flakes into her pots. Mrs Beagle and I enjoy a special relationship because 100% of her time, and about 20% of my time is devoted to the daily task of providing anything up to 160 midday dinners for the children of St. Claude's. Before going on to describe Mrs Beagle's problems I am going to tell you about a few of my own. On the face of it there shouldn't be any. The school dinners accounting system is straightforward and easy to follow.

All primary schools normally accept responsibility for care of the children during the midday lunch break. Therefore, as some children go home for dinner, it is customary for all schools to keep dinner registers which will account for the whereabouts of each child. The registers are divided into columns which allow for the children to be listed and for their dinner intentions to be marked, thus: a tick means the child is staying in for a school dinner (in which case the money – payable in advance at the start of each week – should be entered in the cash column); a letter 'F' means the child is staying in for a school dinner but is entitled to a free one; 'P' means the child has brought a packed lunch to school and will be eating it in that part of the dining hall set aside for such a purpose, and 'H' means the child has gone home. At the end of the week the dinner register of each class should show that the amount of cash paid equals the number of ticks, and the total number of ticks and 'Fs' should equal the number of dinners that Mrs Beagle has provided.

Every day, after completing the attendance register, the class teacher asks each child what it will be doing at lunchtime – and enters an appropriate mark in the dinner register. The dinner register, with tin containing any money collected, will then be sent, in the charge of a responsible pupil, to the school office. When all the dinner registers have arrived upon my desk I add up the total number of dinners required that day and jot it down on a piece of paper to hand to Mrs Beagle. I also tell her of the number of children bringing sandwiches so that she can arrange for tables to be laid accordingly. I keep a separate account, for the benefit of The Authority, of the number of meals both free and paid-for that the school supplies each week, and I submit a termly account to The Authority which proves that I have paid into the local Post Office the correct amount of money to cover those paid meals that Mrs Beagle has supplied. What can go wrong?

I find that each teacher (with the exception of Mr Singleton) presents me with a different sort of problem. With Mrs Snow it is latecomers. Officially our school day starts at 9.00 a.m., but the parents of children in the reception class don't take this seriously. Whilst the working mothers certainly make an early delivery of their children to the playground (sometimes as early as 8.15 a.m.) those mothers who stay at home during the day don't feel any urge to watch the clock. If David has a funny tummy pain, or Deirdre can't find her hair ribbon, or Joseph dawdles over his cornflakes, then the whole family will be late in making a move from home, and the children are delivered to the Reception Class sometimes as late as ten o'clock in the morning. By this time Mrs Snow has already sent her dinner register to the office. If Mrs Snow can catch the parent of a late arrival she will ask them to call at the office to tell me what is happening to the child at lunchtime. But sometimes the parent just opens the door to Mrs Snow's classroom, pushes the child in, and makes off quickly. And sometimes Mrs Snow forgets to tell me about this. At the end of the week Mrs Snow will attach a little note to her dinner register such as: 'On Monday Rachel was late. I marked her absent, but in fact she stayed for dinner that day. The same thing happened with Rachel on Wednesday, and also with Brian on Thursday. Sorry!'

Miss Krantz doesn't allow latecomers. Any parent who tries this trick with her will be pursued across the playground and even into the road by a booming Miss Krantz declaring 'THIS REALLY ISN'T GOOD ENOUGH MRS STOKES. SHIRLEY HAS LOST THREE HOURS OF SCHOOLING ALREADY THIS WEEK BECAUSE OF LATENESS' – and I suspect that those mothers of hers who can't get up in the morning keep their children at home until lunchtime and then bring them along with an excuse like 'James was up all night coughing so I let him lie in this morning' . . . rather than have the embarrassment of being pursued and roared at by Miss Krantz. But Miss Krantz doesn't like collecting dinner money and completing a dinner register. She doesn't think that she should be asked to. 'I'M A TEACHER, NOT A CLERK AND DEBT COLLECTOR' she grumbles, and although her dinner register is neat and without alterations it frequently shows ticks for dinners taken but which haven't been paid for, and I know that it's no good asking Miss Krantz to have a quiet word with the mother when next she sees her. Miss Krantz will refuse . . . 'I'M A TEACHER, NOT A DEBT COLLECTOR!'

I study the ticks gloomily and wonder how difficult it is going to be to actually get the money. Now there probably won't be any difficulty with Mrs A. I know she has a very low income, a family of five, and she spends practically all her money in the supermarket on Saturday morning and so often has very little left on Monday. But her husband gets paid on Fridays, and Mrs A. usually comes in after school to settle up. I shall have to watch Mrs B. and Mrs C. though. No shortage of money there; they just 'never have the change' on a Monday, but I know that if I leave it too long before reminding them they will come in with looks of amazement on their faces . . . 'Surely I don't owe *two weeks* dinner money!' This means I shall have to send notes home to Mrs B. and Mrs C. But Mrs B. is, I think, in France at the moment. And the child of Mrs C. always loses notes on the way home. No wonder I stare gloomily at the ticks in Miss Krantz's register.

Now Mr Scott doesn't mind completing a dinner register, and he cheerfully nags the parents who are unreliable payers; it's just that his register is always wrong. On Fridays a little note will come along to me saying something like this: 'I'm sure Nicholas said he was bringing a packed lunch on Wednesday, but in fact he had a school dinner, and on Thursday I booked a dinner for Jacob who had a hospital appointment and was supposed to be coming back to school but he didn't. I'm afraid I marked Jean absent on Thursday, but she was here - so I suppose she had Jacob's dinner. Anyway – I expect you can sort it out.'

The only complaint I have of Mr Singleton's Dinner Register is that his writing is so small I can barely read it. But all I need to look at is his final total each day. Mr Singleton's register is always correct; what's more he always adds it up and balances out numbers and cash at the end of each week.

Mr Appleby doesn't often make mistakes with his register, but his writing is so bad that *I* frequently make mistakes when trying to read it. In Mr Appleby's scrawl his 'Fs', 'Ps' and 'Hs' look similar. This presents no problem when I know that a certain child *always* has a free dinner, or brings a packed lunch, or goes home. But several of Mr Appleby's children who are entitled to free dinners sometimes bring a packed lunch or go home . . .

You can see from all this that the dinner numbers I jot down on a piece of paper for Mrs Beagle are arbitrary rather than accurate; she can take them as *guidance* only. Fortunately this poses no problems for Mrs Beagle who never seems to run short of dinners, and also has some craftily-tasty ways of dealing with left-overs. Mrs Beagle, one of life's copers, has one guiding principle, and this is that all children shall be fed. She isn't really concerned whether or not the child is entitled to a free dinner, or whether it should have paid but hasn't, or even if it hasn't actually booked a dinner. If a child lines up in front of Mrs Beagle and holds out a plate there will be food put upon it. And if there are squawks from any table that not enough places have been laid, Mrs Beagle will simply chuck some more knives, forks and spoons across the counter and not bother to ask any questions. She knows that we will sort it out on Friday.

Our Friday sort-out is essential. If we wish to avoid awkward questions (and we most certainly do) then Mrs Beagle's monthly account of dinners provided must tie in with my termly account of dinners booked, both free and paid for. On Friday afternoons we have a get-together in her kitchen office cubby-hole and make the appropriate adjustments to our books. I enjoy these Friday half-hours with Mrs Beagle. She usually makes a pot of tea (or, on special occasions like the last day of term, Christmas, or her birthday she will produce a bottle of sherry) and during our Friday Fiddle Session (as Mr Masterton calls it) we can always find time for a sociable gossip and exchange of complaints. And I must admit that Mrs Beagle's problems with The Authority's school meals system make my own whinings about teachers who can't keep dinner registers seem rather trivial.

Mrs Beagle's cookery can't be faulted. Her meat pies are succulent and mouthwatering; her creamy cakes and pastries are greedily attractive. She is also very thoughtful about things like hot plates, and putting aside dinners for staff or children who may be delayed, and she rises generously to special occasions like Christmas, or Summer Fair days. Because of this we are all very fond of her, and tend to overlook minor failings like none-too clean cutlery, and occasional bouts of bad temper. ('The sodding forks have all been through the steriliser' she once roared at Miss Krantz who dared to complain) and we try to ignore the burning cigarette we sometimes see between her fingers as she moves between her office cubby-hole and the kitchen. The Authority, of course, would know nothing of Mrs Beagle's qualities or shortcomings, as a cook. (Visits from The Authority's Catering Manager are rare, and usually notified in advance.) But they are concerned with her bookkeeping and budgeting, and as I know that Mrs Beagle is an accurate and neat keeper of accounts I wouldn't have guessed that she could be in trouble on this score.

I first became aware of Mrs Beagle's battle with The Authority about a year ago when she had a surprise early morning visit from The Authority's Area Catering Supervisor. This lady sat in the office, constantly looking at her watch until five past nine, then said, 'Is Mrs Beagle *always* this late?' I explained that Mrs Beagle often stayed behind in the afternoons to complete her bookwork and I emphasised that she put in far more hours each week than she was paid for. The Area Supervisor was a thin woman with gnarled thin hands, thin lips, and a beige-coloured face. By asking her if I could help I managed to get out of her what she wanted to see Mrs Beagle about. Apparently The Authority is clamping down upon school cooks who don't buy their supplies through The Authority's Consortium – and Mrs Beagle, who always buys her meat and vegetables from the shops near the school, is their most persistent offender. 'But surely,' I said, 'Mrs Beagle always keeps her budget within the allowance made by The Authority for St. Claude's school meals?' 'That's not the point,' the Area Supervisor tapped her clipboard which listed The Authority's Approved Consortium suppliers. 'We get special prices from these people on the understanding that *all* The Authority's schools will order from them. Mrs Beagle has just *got* to conform.' I looked at her in astonishment. 'Are you actually going to tell Mrs Beagle that?' The woman looked surprised., 'Yes, of course. Why?' 'Have you ever met Mrs Beagle?' I enquired. The woman looked even more surprised. 'No. Why?' I didn't have to answer this question because Mrs Beagle herself came in at that point and took over the conversation. Grasping the situation immediately she gave the woman an oily smile and suggested that the interview should be continued in her kitchen. 'A pity you people don't come and see us cooks more often,' she said falsely as she led the Catering Supervisor away.

I never got to hear the full story of the row that followed. It seems that Mrs Beagle's display of friendly co-operation didn't last long and that voices were raised and bad language used. All I know is that after about twenty minutes the Area Catering Supervisor came back through the office with a face now rather more pink than beige – and that Mrs Beagle was in a foul mood all morning. But during the following Friday fiddle session she told me that she had failed to get permission to continue using the local butcher and greengrocer. 'So you can expect a right balls-up with the meals in future,' she said.

It must have been a sad day for the local butcher and greengrocer when Mrs Beagle told them that they could no longer have the school's custom. A happy working relationship, built up over the years, had come to an end. Perhaps this was what The Authority wanted. Perhaps they didn't want 'happy working relationships' developing between school cooks and the local traders. Because of Mrs Beagle's contacts the school had always been supplied with good fresh meat and vegetables on the day and at the hour she wanted them. Whether or not the butcher and greengrocer 'saw that she was all right' as a result of this custom I don't know. (They certainly 'saw that the school was all right' on the occasions we went begging for contributions towards our Summer Fair and Christmas Bazaar.) All I know is that the shopkeepers were happy; Mrs Beagle was happy; and the school was happy. As Mrs Beagle never overspent, The Authority should have been happy. But they weren't, and now Mrs Beagle has to telephone her orders for meat and vegetables to large suppliers whose depots are twenty miles distant and who frequently let her down ('the lorry drivers are on strike' . . . 'the road is blocked with snow' . . . 'there's a new driver on and he couldn't find your school' . . . 'your pork was offloaded at another school by mistake so you'll have to make do with sausages'). What's more it seems to me that the opportunity for 'making a bit on the side' has not been removed from the system, it has just moved a little further up the hierarchy. The first firm contracted to supply vegetables to all schools was reasonably efficient, and Mrs Beagle had few complaints. Then, without warning, the contract was given to another firm who proved to be unreliable and uncaring, and who supplied rotting potatoes, mouldering cauliflowers, limp root vegetables and who ignored all complaints. Why were they given the contract? Mrs Beagle wonders; and so do I.

Another problem Mrs Beagle has with The Authority is that they turn a deaf ear to her requests for things she urgently needs (like a new plastic draining rack – some replacement gravy spoons – or the repair of her washing machine) but they insist upon her having things that she doesn't need – like the new £7,000 chip frying unit they installed during the Easter holidays last year. Mrs Beagle didn't want a new 'chipper'. She was perfectly happy with her old one. However she was told that this money had been 'allocated' to her kitchen and that she must have a new chipper because her old one was 'obsolete'. Mrs Beagle daily mourns the loss of her old trouble-free cast-iron chipper. The new gleaming sheet-steel one gets so hot it burns the front of her legs as she stands in front of it, and it is always going wrong.

But in spite of all these difficulties there has been no deterioration in Mrs Beagle's cooking. She continues to produce enticing meals in her robust, motherly fashion. But she is looking rather exasperated these days, and has to spend a lot of time making long telephone calls in pursuit of goods that haven't arrived, or jobs in the kitchen that haven't been attended to. What's more, for the first time ever, she is now talking of early retirement. 'It's not the job it was,' she said recently. 'They don't need real cooks any more; just people to open cans, and mix water with powdered muck.'

With the increase in control from The Authority there

has come an increase of paperwork flowing into Mrs Beagle's kitchen. Almost daily a large envelope comes addressed to the Kitchen Manageress and it contains Price Lists, 'Health & Safety' documents, long letters about fire hazards and legal matters, and a jolly little paper called 'Cookscorner' which gives stirring homilies about the 'rewarding work we are all engaged upon', friendly news about ladies who are leaving to have babies, and cheerful little poems made up by happy kitchen staff – alongside the details of redundancy terms agreed by The Authority, and the lists of injuries received by careless workers. Apart from the documents dealing with current food prices (which she pins up on her notice board) I don't think Mrs Beagle reads any of it. The Health & Safety regulations she shoves into a drawer; the Cookscorner paper she puts aside for her Kitchen Assistants to read, and the rest goes into the wastepaper basket. 'If I stopped to look at this lot,' she once said, 'I'd never get dinner cooked.'

Mrs Beagle's notice board makes interesting reading Through studying her pinned-up information sheets last week I was able to learn that Green Streak, Green Fore and the Unibit 207.14 mince extender were up in price and that it was now recommended to use milk powder with Edifas when making 'whipped cream'. Under the heading 'Kitchen Swill' I read a sad little message that Mr Butterworth who normally collected The Authority's swill had taken early retirement and that the new holder of the Kitchen Swill Contract was a Mr Heap. There was an enthusiastic write-up on a new product called Unimills T.V.P. (I was unable to gather whether Mrs Beagle should cook it, or clean the stove with it) but my curiosity was really aroused by a cryptic little note from The Authority informing Mrs Beagle that St. Claude's had now been designated as an Emergency Feeding Station and that she should take great care of the Yellow Booklet supplied for her information. 'What's all this about?' I asked her. Mrs Beagle removed the letter from her notice board. 'I shouldn't really have pinned that up,' she said, 'it's supposed to be hush-hush,' – and she then told me all about it.

Certain school kitchens, it seems, have been designated by The Authority as Emergency Feeding Stations so that in the event of a National Emergency (and no-one has yet dared mention The Emergency they have in mind) the local populace will have a place where they can gather and be fed. The kitchens so designated must have certain structural alterations made but, in the meantime, each cook affected by this plan must set aside a store-cupboard which must be stocked with Authority-Approved Emergency Food. Full details of the scheme are given in the Yellow Booklet which must be kept in a safe and secret place. 'But they've never sent me the bloody thing,' said Mrs Beagle, 'which is why I had the note pinned up – to remind me to keep reminding them.' However, Mrs Beagle had already set aside her Emergency Cupboard and I asked to have a peep inside. 'Oh, until they send me the details I'm using it as a temporary dumping ground,' she explained. I opened the cupboard door and was not reassured by what I saw. I only hope that Mrs Beagle receives her Yellow Booklet from The Authority before the coming of the holocaust, otherwise the survivors of the St. Claude's area who gather in the kitchen for nourishment will be fed upon 24 packets of Angel Whirl, a drum of Dream Topping and two crates of 'Crusha' milk shake syrup.

Every now and then one of The Authority's accountants will drop in at the school to examine our account books. The Authority employs a whole team of travelling accountants upon this sort of work and we rarely get the same one twice. Some of them are stern, with penetrating beady eyes that make me feel very guilty and cause me to fumble with pages, drop tins of cash all over the floor and even (on one occasion) forget the number combination to open the safe. But sometimes they are jolly fellows prepared to flip through my books, initial them in green ink, and then sit and chat over a cup of coffee. Reckoning that these chaps must be in the know about everything that goes on at the Education Office I usually try to get them talking about various aspects of The Authority's finances – and we usually come back to the same subject: that is, the appalling cost of providing midday meals for schoolchildren. Just think, for example, of the number of schools in *your* county – and think of the cooks, kitchen assistants, dining-room assistants and school meals

101

supervisory assistants employed to provide a school meal service. And just think, as well, of the free meals that the Local Authority supplies. (About one-third of the St. Claude's children have free dinners.) Whilst the principle of supplying poor hungry children with free meals is a good and proper one, the system is sometimes abused. Many of the St. Claude's free mealers are neither poor nor hungry, but have parents who have found out how to manipulate the rules.

Two of our children receiving free meals have parents who are occasionally seen riding around in a Volvo car and who fly to Sri Lanka twice a year in order to visit their Guru. These transcontinental jaunts greatly upset the Educational Welfare Officer who organises the free meal tickets (he drives a Mini and can only afford Bournemouth for his holidays) but as the family are in receipt of social security and family income supplement they are automatically entitled to free school meals. Teachers who do a 'dinner duty' (and this can mean anything from running a lunchtime club to just sitting at table with the children) are also entitled to a free meal. (Anyone who considers this to be a 'perk' has obviously never dined with a group of junior children who are shovelling sponge and custard into their mouths, flicking peas around the room, or spitting their food back onto their plates for re-investigation. And there will always be at least one child in desperate need of a handkerchief.)

But all these costs are just the tip of the iceberg. What about the school secretary's time in every school, the overheads and administration costs for the dozens of Catering Supervisors for each area, and the training kitchens. What about the courses run at Catering Training Colleges? How much does it cost, I wonder, to equip and maintain all these school kitchens? What about the enormous cost of fuel? How many clerks are employed to check and 'process' school meals documents, and, coming back full circle to my friendly chatting accountant, how much of *his* time is spent on such matters? As the children are usually receiving education for five hours of the school day, why could not things be rearranged so that they started school at 8.00 a.m. and went home, having finished with schooling for the day, at 1.30. This would allow for a half-hour's playtime mid-morning, and would put the responsibility of feeding children back into the hands of their parents. Wouldn't this be a good idea? But no-one agrees with me. I am urged to think of all the unemployment this would cause – not only of those concerned with providing the meals, but also of those mothers who would have to give up their jobs in order to care for their children each afternoon. 'Your suggestion would threaten the very fabric of our society!' one chatting accountant assured me dramatically. 'The benevolent concept of feeding children midday is not so important these days, but keeping the whole administrative machinery going most certainly is.'

I once tried to impress a friendly visiting accountant with the imaginative and unorthodox methods I use in order to keep my end of the 'administrative machinery' going. He seemed a particularly jocular sort of chap, so when he asked me the usual final question '. . . and now may I count up all the cash you have in the school?' I asked him flippantly whether he would like to see my unders-and-overs bag. 'Your *what*?' he said. So I explained. Let us assume, for example, that in one week John, Diana and Paul will each, on separate occasions, forget that they were supposed to be going home and instead go up to the hall for a dinner. Mrs Beagle will give them one – not knowing that they haven't been ordered. John, Diana and Paul have honest mothers who, on realising what has happened, will (sometimes the following week) come along to the office and offer me the extra dinner money, which I have no way of recording because, according to my books and Mrs Beagle's books John, Diana and Paul did not have those dinners. However, it being right and proper that they should pay for the dinners they didn't officially have (are you still with me?) I put the money into my unders-and-overs bag.

My friendly accountant was looking a little perturbed at this stage and started to fold up his books, muttering something about it not being wise to tell him any more. 'Ah, but it doesn't end there,' I insisted, 'because the same thing can happen in reverse. John can, perhaps, be sent home from school just before dinner because he's not very well, Diana's mother may telephone to book a dinner –

saying that Diana has an early appointment with the dentist but will want her dinner but, in the event, the visit to the dentist is too upsetting for her and she doesn't in fact come to school that day – and possibly Paul's teacher will tick him in for dinner by mistake when in fact he brought a packed lunch. My books will show that all three children had dinners which must be paid for; the parents won't want to pay for dinners the children haven't eaten, and so I square the accounts by taking the money from my unders-and-overs bag.' My friendly accountant hurriedly shoved all his books into his briefcase. 'I do not wish to see your unders-and-overs bag; I do not wish to hear any more about it; you can forget you told me.' But a further thought troubled him, and as he reached the door he turned and asked, 'As a matter of curiosity, how much money is currently involved in this, er, system?' 'Oh, we're doing quite well at the moment,' I said, 'I've got just over £14.00 in hand.' He muttered something that sounded like 'Jesus Christ!' . . . and fled.

CHAPTER SEVEN

The School Governors

The Governors of St. Claude's hold a meeting at the school once a term, and I attend these meetings in order to take the Minutes. They are important occasions. When the date of a meeting is chosen it is circled in red upon my calendar, and as it approaches I give Mr Potts a reminder so that on the evening before he can arrange to polish the corridor and scrub fingermarks off the main entrance door. On the day itself Mr Masterton will come to school wearing his best suit, Mrs Beagle will bake a selection of cream cakes and almond buns to serve to the Governors with the afternoon tea, and Mrs Potts will give a final rub to the corridor floor and squirt 'fresh-aire' spray in the vicinity of the boys' toilets. As the meeting time approaches I will lay out pads of paper and sharpened pencils on the table in the library, and Miss Krantz will arrange the flowers. Whilst the meeting is in progress Mr Appleby doesn't let his class do any metalwork or woodwork – and two monitors are stationed each end of the corridor to prevent children from running past the library door.

The meetings follow a pattern which has not varied in all the years I have been taking the Minutes. (I have frequently been able to produce identical Agendas on several successive occasions.) Apologies for absence will be followed by the acceptance and signing of the Minutes of the last meeting and the discussion of any matters arising from them. Then Mr Masterton reads his Report. In this report he will give the numbers of children currently on roll and the numbers of those staying to school dinners. He will describe events which have taken place in the school, and list those that are about to happen. Questions are asked; answers given, and then we move on to the next item which is correspondence. Here Mr Masterton will produce any letters received from The Authority which he feels should be brought to the Governors' attention. The date of the next meeting is decided upon, and then we finally move to Any Other Business.

But although the pattern of the meetings has remained unchanged for the last ten years, the *tone* of the meetings is changing rapidly. In the early days I could happily doze away over my pad in the corner of the library knowing that the Minutes I would eventually produce would be very similar to the last lot and that no-one would argue about them anyway. But this is not the case these days. Now I have to keep my wits about me and be fully aware of what is going on. Most of the old school Governors are gone, and the new ones are an entirely different breed. I believe that these changes at St. Claude's reflect a nationwide trend of school governors' posts being taken over by academic people of left-wing politics – a trend which is causing a lot of worry in some quarters. 'A Red Threat to our Schools' screamed the headline in our local newspaper recently . . . 'Commie Governors use wrecking tactics at School Meetings' said another.

If the Governing Bodies of our schools are now being dominated by political activists, does this in fact mean that our schools are coming under a malign influence? And should we be doing something about it? If I describe to you what used to happen in the old days – and what is now happening – you can judge the extent of the danger for yourself.

With the exception of the posts of Parent-Governor and Teacher-Governor, most of the Governors of St. Claude's had been in office for about fifteen years until the last elections. Mrs Glugburn (Chairman) is a retired professional cellist and lives in a large Georgian house near the school, at the top of the hill. She has a forceful go-getting personality and is actively concerned with the local Community Association. She is a competent nagger of the local Council, and gets things done like repairs to pavements and filling-in-of potholes. She attends all school concerts and is a particularly enthusiastic supporter of Mr Singleton's Early Music Group. She has given a small silver cup to the school (The Glugburn Trophy) which is awarded each year to the young musician who 'gives the most talented performance'. Major Darnall (Vice-Chairman) has lived all his life in the St. Claude's area and owns a lot of property around The Hill. He can always be relied upon to find a bed-sitter for a student, or a vacant flat for a needy family. He is a jovial man and each year plays the part of St. Claude's Father Christmas – spending the whole afternoon togged up in red robes, white beard and wellington boots, giving out presents to the infant children. (He always donates a large cheque to help pay for the contents of his sack of toys.)

Mrs Glugburn and Major Darnall still serve as Governors to St. Claude's school, but the other previously long-standing officers, who have since been ousted, are Mr Derby – a quiet man who owns a bookshop and who always gives us a special discount on books and also presents several books each year to the St. Claude's library; Mr Bender – who owns a mini-bus firm and who is particularly keen on encouraging sporting activities for boys (he used to give us free use of a mini-bus for each class outing); and old Mrs Bennett. Mrs Bennett has lived all her long life near the school. She used to own a grocer's shop down on the main road and she knows everyone in the area. Her particular concern over the years has been the physical well-being of the children. But she is now very deaf, has a bad leg, and although she attended all meetings regularly she never took much part, other than to ask occasionally if Mr Masterton was sure the children were getting enough to eat.

The other two Governors' posts are those of Parent-Governor (elected by paper ballot, organised by the PTA) and Teacher-Governor. The teacher-governor is theoretically elected by ballot amongst the teaching staff, but it's a job that nobody wants and Miss Krantz has been persuaded, albeit with much grumbling, to do it because she lives nearest to the school and would be the least inconvenienced by having to attend meetings, which sometimes do run on a bit. Our present parent-governor is Mrs Richardson. She was elected when the post was created five years ago, and her daughter Venetia Richardson was in the reception class. Mrs Richardson is likely to remain the parent-governor for some time yet because she is popular with other parents and although Venetia will be passing on to secondary education at the end of this year her sister, little Felicity, is now in Mrs Snow's class. As these two 'special' governors' posts are filled by elections supervised by the school, any gerrymandering would be difficult to organise – and Miss Krantz and Mrs Richardson both kept their appointments at the last re-shuffle.

In order to demonstrate the differences between the old Governors' Meetings and the new, I am going to pretend that a tape recorder was set to work during one of the meetings and you are now about to read a transcript of part of the tape. Let us assume, therefore, that the meeting started at two o'clock as usual; the first two items on the agenda have been dealt with, and Mr Masterton is now reading his report:

Mr Masterton: ' . . . 160 children in the school and about 150 of them stay to school dinner. 54 of them are entitled to free meals. 60 infants are having milk each day and . . .'

Mrs Bennett: 'Why aren't the juniors having milk?'

Mrs Glugburn: 'Oh that was stopped years ago Mrs B. Don't you remember – the fuss we made about it when they decided to cut out milk for the juniors?'

Mrs Bennett: 'Well, they shouldn't have. Growing children ought to have milk – look at the energy some of those boys put out.'

Mr Masterton: 'Yes, well, in spite of not having free milk, you'll be pleased to know that our football team, under Mr Appleby's enthusiastic guidance, won four games out of the seven fixtures last term. Also, I'm pleased to say that St. Claude's again took part in the City Schools Carol Festival at Christmas. You will be interested to hear that one of Mr Singleton's girls won a prize in the Post Office 'Write a Letter' competition, and also several children from Mr Scott's class submitted entries to the Cadbury's poster painting competition. Turning now to . . .'

Mrs Bennett: 'Mr Scott – that's the new teacher. How's he settling in?'

Mr Masterton: 'Well, he's actually been with us nearly two years now; it's amazing how time flies.'

Mrs Bennett: 'Is he related to the family that used to keep the post office stores down on the main road?'

Major Darnall: 'Ah, you're thinking of Mr and Mrs *Short*, who kept the post office.'

Mrs Bennett: 'Well, they had a son who went to university. Married that girl who was dinner lady at Commercial Street.'

Major Darnall: 'Yes dear – but the name was *Short*.'

Mrs Glugburn: 'I do think we ought to move on now and hear the rest of Mr Masterton's report.'

(Mr Masterton then continues reading his report without further interruption.)

Mrs Glugburn: 'Well, that was a most interesting report. It is *so* good to hear that St. Claude's is encouraging all the artistic and academic abilities of our children. I think a special Minute should be made recording our appreciation to Mr Masterton.'

(general burble of consent from Governors)

Mrs Glugburn: 'Now the next item on the Agenda is Correspondence. Have you anything to report to us, Mr Masterton?'

Mrs Bennett: '*Short.*'

Mrs Glugburn: 'What was that dear?'

Mrs Bennett: '*Short* – I've now remembered – the post office people were called *Short* – but they did have a boy who became a teacher; I expect he would be about Mr Scott's age.'

Major Darnall (leaning over and patting Mrs Bennett's hand, and hissing loudly into her ear); 'I think Mr Masterton is about to read us a letter from the Director of Education.'

(Mrs Bennett sighs and leans back in her chair)

Mr Masterton: 'You may remember we wrote last year to complain that the school urgently needed redecoration, and that at the last meeting we decided to write again as no reply had been received. Well, at last we've got a very long letter from the Director which I don't think you'll actually want me to read, but the gist of it is that he says money can't be allocated for redecorating works at the moment.'

Mrs Richardson: 'Well, I think that's disgusting; something at least should be done about the infant's toilets. Can't we insist that something is done because of the *health risk*?'

(At this point Mrs Bennett falls asleep)

Major Darnall: 'Keep on nagging them! It's the only thing to do. Perhaps we all ought to write individual letters. Quote the Health and Safety Act at them; that'll shift them.'

(A general discussion follows and it is decided that Mrs Glugburn writes a strongly-worded protest about the Director's decision and asks again that 'reconsideration be given to the painting of the infants' toilet block'.

Mrs Glugburn: 'Well now, we're making quite good time. Any Other Business. Has anyone any point they wish to discuss?'

Mr Bender: 'Yes. I know I've said it before, but I want to make the point again. The gymnasium equipment at this school is just not good enough. It's downright scruffy; probably not safe either.'

(Several Governors sigh. Mr Bender always brings up the subject of the gymnasium equipment under Any Other Business.)

Mrs Glugburn: 'Well, if they won't allow money to redecorate the infants' toilets I can't see them spending it on gym equipment.'

Mr Bender: 'Well, what about the Health and Safety Act for this one too? I really think . . .'

(A rattle of a tea trolley outside the door causes everyone to sit up suddenly and look cheerful. Major Darnall gently pats Mrs Bennett's hand again, and then Mrs Beagle sweeps in. The tea trolley is spread with a clean white cloth and bears a large tea pot, the best tea-service, and jugs of milk and hot water. But everyone's eyes turn to the bottom shelf of the trolley where the cakes are. The centrepiece is a gateau – fluffy with nut-decorated cream at the sides and glistening with chocolate-decorated lemon curd on top. On either side of the gateau are plates of almond, cherry and raisin-enriched Danish pastries; jam doughnuts (obviously still a little warm) and large cream puffs. Mrs Beagle is wearing a clean white nylon overall and an ingratiating smile. There is now a general buzz of conversation. Mrs Richardson asks Mrs Glugburn if she would like a few tomato plants as they have brought on rather too many this year; Mr Bender has a polite ear cocked towards Mrs Bennett who is still remembering the Short family, and Miss Krantz is complaining to Major Darnall about an AWFUL FAMILY who have recently moved into one of his flats near her house. Mrs Beagle moves amongst us handing out cups of tea and plates of cakes – her face flushing pinkly at the spontaneous (but expected) compliments on her cookery. Mr Derby (who hasn't said anything throughout the whole meeting) selects a small Danish pastry which he cuts very carefully into four pieces before eating. Mrs Beagle leaves us with the trolley and the remains of the tea and cakes and she bows her way out to the accompaniment of many expressions of congratulations and thanks. The general conversation continues for a while until Mrs Glugburn raises her voice to catch everyone's attention.)

Mrs Glugburn: 'Well, I do really think we ought to get on now; there's a very important matter regarding the children's play area at the bottom of the hill I want to bring up.'

Mr Bender: 'You mean those yobbos that go roaring through it on motor bikes some evenings. I rang the Police about it the other night.'

Mrs Glugburn: 'I am *always* ringing the Police about it – but by the time they arrive the motor bikes have gone. I think the Council ought to do something about it by railing off the area in such a way that motor bikes can't get through to it; so I propose that a letter from the Governors of St. Claude's School be sent . . .'

(In the general discussion that followed everyone agrees with Mrs Glugburn, who says she will write the letter on behalf of the St. Claude's Governing Body. Mrs Glugburn then declares the meeting closed, and I shut my shorthand notebook and gather up my papers. Mr Bender and Major Darnall help Mrs Bennett out of her chair and they pick up her walking stick and handbag from the floor and put them into her hands. They discuss which one of them is going to take her home – and decide that as Mr Bender has brought the Mini today it had better be Major Darnall because his Chrysler will provide more leg room for Mrs Bennett. Mrs

Glugburn leaves with Mrs Richardson; Mr Derby has a quiet word with Mr Masterton before slipping away, and Miss Krantz – who joins me in gathering up the scattered teacups – helps herself to the last piece of gateau remaining on the plate. Miss Krantz then returns to her classroom, and I push the trolley up to the kitchen to help Mrs Beagle wash up. It is now 3.25 p.m. and in five minutes' time the going-home bell will be rung.)

This used to be the pattern of St. Claude's Governors' Meetings term after term after term.

School Governors keep their seats of office for five years and then there are re-elections. I have never been able to find out how these elections are organised. (When I put this question to the girl in The Authority's office that deals with such things she said: 'I don't know; we just get notified who the new school governors are – and then I notify you.') In the term that follows the end of a five-year period all schools have to wait to receive the Official Notification from The Authority to learn who the new governors are. In the past there have been few surprises; and absences caused by death or resignation of a Governor will be filled by a new name but, until this last occasion, the new person generally had some sort of link with the school. When I opened the Official Notification last time I stared at it in astonishment. Mrs Glugburn and Major Darnall were still there – but who on earth were Bernard Dyer, Justin Pugh and Ms Hilary Fang? And where were Mr Derby, Mr Bender and old Mrs Bennett? I consulted with Mr Masterton. He hadn't heard of any of the new Governors – and noted that none of them lived anywhere near our part of the city. I telephoned The Authority and was informed that Governors Dyer, Pugh and Fang were all Labour nominations. Mr Masterton telephoned Mrs Glugburn who couldn't think of any reason for such an upheaval and suggested, worriedly, that *something was going on*. The Head of Commercial Street School rang Mr Masterton in a panic. His entire Governing Body had been replaced by strangers. St. Jude's School (across the water from us) weren't so badly off. When I rang them the secretary told me that only four of their governors had been replaced by Labour nominees but at their first meeting the Vicar had been unseated from his office as Chairman – a position he had held for the previous 17 years. Our first meeting was due to be held in three weeks' time. Mr Masterton and I awaited it anxiously.

In the meantime we were reading in our local newspapers that the events at St. Claude's, Commercial Street and St. Jude's were, in fact, being repeated in schools (both primary and secondary) all over the country. The new 'left-wing' Governors, we read, were out to disrupt meetings by constantly querying the Head's Report, asking unexpected questions, demanding meetings at awkward times, using 'filibustering' on unimportant matters to exasperate other non-member Governors, and repeatedly demanding extra meetings on obscure topics. The bit I didn't like was the suggestion that these new Governors were going to 'seek to discredit the Clerk; question the accuracy of the Minutes and constantly query points of procedure' . . . I could see that my days of dozing over my pad in the library were over. However, as things turned out, the first meeting of the new Governing Body was a bit of an anti-climax. I don't really know what I was expecting, but the three new Governors who took their places around the table in the library seemed to be quite ordinary people. They were polite and smiling, and we all exchanged normal comments about the weather – and cautiously investigated each other's backgrounds with phrases like . . . 'And have you ever been to the St. Claude's area before?' . . . or 'Have you been working at the school for long?'

The first meeting of the new Governors of a school is usually a short, formal one, dealing with the nominations of a Chairman and a Vice-Chairman. Politics had never before featured in any of the St. Claude's meetings (although the Tories obviously predominated) but now we had an interesting line-up of Governors Dyer, Pugh and Fang (Lab.), Darnall and Richardson (Con.) and Glugburn (late Lib. but now SDP). (Mr Masterton has never shown obvious support for any of the parties.) Our meeting started at the usual time of 2.00 p.m. and everyone was very polite. Mrs Glugburn was returned as Chairman without any difficulty. There was a slight skirmish over the election of Vice-Chairman, when Mr Dyer suggested it might be appropriate for a new Governor to take this

113

position, but he was out-voted and Major Darnall was returned again.

When Mrs Beagle brought in the tea trolley I noticed our new Governors staring in amazement at the creamy and colourful array of cakes on the bottom shelf. Mr Dyer said, 'I see you believe in doing things properly here at St. Claude's,' and Ms Fang smiled delightedly as she lifted an extra large piece of gateau onto her plate. Two doughnuts and three cups of tea later, she was telling me about the children's drama school she was hoping to set up, and I was sympathising with her over the difficulties she was experiencing as an out-of-work supply teacher. 'There just aren't any permanent posts available in this damned county,' she said. Mr Dyer began talking to Major Darnall about cars – and I heard Mr Pugh telling Mrs Richardson and Mrs Glugburn about the new Nature Trail he hoped to establish in the inner-city area. I was beginning to relax and think that the newspapers had, as usual exaggerated everything, when we came to the point of deciding the date and time of the next meeting. All three newcomers claimed that 2.00 p.m. in the afternoon was most inconvenient for them and could we meet in future at 9.00 a.m. This took the rest of us by surprise, and as no-one could immediately think of a valid reason for refusing this request, the time of 9.00 a.m. was decided upon. (My first thought had been 'Who's going to add up the dinner registers if I'm in here taking minutes?' but I decided to say nothing and to put the problem to Mr Masterton when the time came.)

In the event, the 9.00 a.m. meeting idea was a short-lived one. Although Mr Appleby agreed to take on the job of sorting out the dinner registers, no similar attitude of flexibility was forthcoming from Mrs Beagle. 'Please yourself what time you hold your bloody meeting,' she said, 'but don't expect me to bring in the trolley. When I'm in the middle of dinners I can't fart-ass around making cakes for you lot!' The meeting started promptly, as arranged, with everyone present. It was a slow long-drawn-out one. There were a lot of questions asked. Not very awkward ones – just a lot of them. As 10.00 a.m. passed, and then 11.00 a.m., and someone muttered something about 'refreshment', Mr Masterton explained that we couldn't interrupt Mrs Beagle while she was preparing school dinners and that perhaps we had just better 'press on'. When we came to the item on the Agenda 'Date and time of next meeting' I am sure that the happy memory of Mrs Beagle and her trolley influenced the decision, and our three new Governors found that they could, after all, in future meet at 2.00 p.m. We had been sitting in a rather hot library for well over $2\frac{1}{2}$ hours and when Mrs Glugburn said she assumed that no-one had Any Other Business to discuss, nobody disagreed with her.

Since then our Governor's Meetings have fallen back into their old 2.00 p.m. routine, pleasantly interrupted by Mrs Beagle wheeling in the tea and cakes. We are gradually learning something about our new Governors (Mr Dyer, married with one daughter, is a lecturer at the University School of Medicine, and Mr Pugh is something in the Museum world) but although our casual conversation over the tea cups is friendly enough, there is a very guarded relationship between the old order and the new during the formal part of the meetings. To illustrate this let us go back to our tape-recorded meeting – substituting the new Governors for the old.

Mr Masterton is reading his report:

Mr Masterton: '. . . 160 children in the school and about 150 of them stay to . . .'

Mr Dyer: 'According to the last Minutes we had 165 children in the school; do we know where those 5 children have gone?'

Mr Masterton (looking at me): 'Yes, of course we do, er . . .'

Me: 'This was a family of five children that have now moved to the north of England.' (It wasn't. I couldn't remember, any more than Mr Masterton could, where those five children had gone, and I didn't have my Removal Register with me. But I knew that Mr Dyer was just making his usual interruptions and that a prompt answer would satisfy him.)

Mr Masterton (continuing): '150 stay to dinner. 54 of them are entitled to free meals. 60 infants are . . .'

Mr Dyer: 'That's quite a high proportion of children having free meals. I trust they aren't made to feel any *different* from the children who pay for them. How do you ensure that the children who *pay* don't know about the free ones?'

Mr Masterton: 'All the staff are most discreet about this. I can assure you that we don't have any problems on that score.'

(We don't either. No 'discreet' member of staff is going to prevent our 54 cheerfully boasting free-mealers from announcing their privileged status to their peers. I have known one or two mothers sensitive about this matter but never a child.)

Mr Masterton (continuing): 'You'll be pleased to know that our football team, under Mr Appleby's enthusiastic guidance, won four games out of the . . .'

Ms Fang: 'How many girls in your football team?'

Mr Masterton: 'Girls? Why, er, none.'

Ms Fang: 'Why not? I trust there is no sexist reason which prevents them joining in?'

Mr Masterton: 'Good Heavens no. I suppose if a girl wanted to play football there's no reason why she shouldn't, but our girls prefer netball.'

Ms Fang: 'What about metalwork and woodwork? Or are you going to tell me that your girls prefer needlework and cookery?'

Miss Krantz: 'I CAN ASSURE YOU THAT IN MY CLASS CHILDREN ARE TREATED AS LITTLE *PEOPLE:* THE BOYS ARE ENCOURAGED TO DO COOKERY JUST AS MUCH AS THE GIRLS.'

Mr Masterton: 'All the children at St. Claude's are encouraged in all subjects, and you have no reason to fear any discrimination because of sex.'

Mrs Glugburn: 'Can Mr Masterton carry on with his report now. We've rather a lot to get through.'

Mr Masterton (continuing): 'Once again St. Claude's took part in the City Schools Carol Festival at Christmas and you will be interested to hear . . .'

Mr Dyer: 'I've been meaning to ask you about religion. What exactly happens in your religious assemblies? I would be a bit worried if I thought the children were being indoctrinated into any specific religious beliefs.'

Major Darnall: '*Indoctrinated!* I've never heard such rubbish. Surely, it's our duty to give the children some decent Christian guidance.'

Mr Masterton: 'I think no-one need worry on this score. Our assemblies always contain a *moral message* but it's not necessarily a *Christian* message, except, of course, at Christmas time.'

Mrs Glugburn: 'I really feel, Mr Dyer, that this should have been brought up under Any Other Business. Can we let Mr Masterton finish his report now?'

Mr Masterton (continuing): 'You will be interested to hear that one of Mr Singleton's girls won a prize in the Post Office 'Write a Letter' competition, and also several children from Mr Scott's class submitted entries to the Cadbury's poster painting competition. Turning now to . . .'

Mr Pugh: 'I'm somewhat surprised, Madam Chairman, that the school encourages the children to take part in competitions when it is an educationally acknowledged fact that a competitive spirit amongst the children is not necessarily a good thing.'

Mrs Richardson: 'But Mr Pugh, the children *enjoy* these competitions. I know that my eldest girl Venetia gets great excitement from the painting competition.'

Mr Pugh (smiling thinly): 'Yes, I'm quite sure that an *able* child would enjoy entering a competition; but surely, the inadequate child is made to feel even more of a failure – either by entering the competition and repeatedly failing, or by avoiding the competition altogether. I'm not saying they're a bad thing – but just that the *school* shouldn't be organising them.'

(In this way Mr Masterton continues to limp patiently through his report. If the idea behind these constant interruptions is to annoy the other Governors, then it certainly works with Major Darnall and Mrs Glugburn – both of whom are looking distinctly rattled by the time Mr Masterton has finished.)

Mrs Glugburn: 'Now the next item on the Agenda is Correspondence. Have you anything to report to us, Mr Masterton?'

Mr Masterton: 'Yes, we have at last had a reply from the Director. You may remember that at the meeting before last we decided to write to complain of the rather large classes each teacher is taking, and to request a re-examination of our teaching-time allocation as we felt we should be entitled to at least 5/10ths extra staff. At the last meeting we decided to write again as no reply had been received. Well, at last we've got a very long letter from the Director which I don't think you'll actually want me to read – but the gist of it is that he says due to a policy decision with regard to the cutting of teaching posts within the County, no extra staff can be allowed at St. Claude's. He suggests that, with a falling pupil roll situation, the position should ease at the end of the academic year when 22 of our children move on to secondary education.'

(There is a general burst of indignant noise at this announcement.)

Ms Fang: 'Well that's absolutely disgusting. There are around 32 children in each class. Doesn't the stupid sod know that no reception class should contain more than 26 infants?'

Mr Pugh (sniggering): 'I don't think that last remark should be minuted.'

Ms Fang: 'Oh, I don't know . . . let the old fool know what we think of him.'

Miss Krantz: 'I DON'T THINK YOU ARE ABSOLUTELY CORRECT ACTUALLY: THE LIMIT OF 26 IS ONLY AN NUT RECOMMENDATION: IT'S NOT LEGISLATIVE YOU KNOW.'

(Miss Krantz has been taking up the challenge of these new Governors and she is making sure she is absolutely up-to-date on all Union matters.)

Mr Pugh: 'We could try writing to the Press. There's nothing The Authority dislikes more than an open letter of complaint from school governors.'

(A general discussion follows and a final decision made that Mrs Glugburn will write again to the Director of Education, mentioning the recommended limit of 26 pupils for the Reception Class, as it was felt that the hint of 'Union trouble' might have some effect. The rattle of a tea trolley outside the door causes everyone to sit up suddenly and look cheerful. But Mrs Glugburn doesn't allow the conversation to drift for long during tea-time. She knows that the longest and most argumentative items on the Agenda will come up under Any Other Business and so, as soon as Mrs Beagle leaves the room, she brings the meeting together again.)

Mrs Glugburn: 'Well now. Any Other Business. Who wants to speak first?'

Mr Pugh: 'Well, I would like to put forward a proposal for consideration by the Meeting that this school takes part in the Official Peace Education Project by introducing Peace Education into the curriculum, and . . .'

Major Darnall: 'What!'

Mr Pugh: 'If I might continue . . . I understand that the Local Authority has agreed to run courses for teaching staff on the subject and there is an exhibition which can be hired by schools. This contains material on such vital issues as the nuclear arms race, war and violence – also non-violence in action, pacifism and peacemaking. The entire project . . .'

Major Darnall: 'But this is absolutely ludicrous and against all normal school principles. On no account can we allow our children to be exposed to political indoctrination.'

Mr Dyer: '*Indoctrination*? Surely, Major, as with religious beliefs, it is our duty to give the children some . . . "decent guidance" were the words I think you used?'

Major Darnall: 'That's entirely beside the point. Mr Pugh is talking politics – and there is no place for that on a primary school curriculum.'

Mr Pugh: 'As I haven't yet been allowed to speak I think you are pre-judging the question. If I may continue I will describe the basis of the project. The course for teachers is in seven parts. These are Violence in Action – ranging from the physical to the psychological (for example family rows, rights, etc.) – then violence within the education system – then the violence of different political systems – capitalism, communism, fascism and . . .'

(Mr Pugh lectures us for nearly 20 minutes, going into the seven Peace Project points in detail. Mr Dyer and Ms Fang listen to him earnestly; Mr Dyer giving a nod of approval every now and then. I can see also, from Mrs Richardson's expression, that she is struggling to give the proposal a fair hearing. The others just watch Mr Pugh in stony silence.

Eventually the proposal is put to the Meeting – and defeated.)

Mrs Glugburn (wearily): 'Is there any other business?'

Mr Dyer: 'Well actually my point follows on to what Mr Pugh has been saying. You will all have read in the Press that many local Authorities are banning corporal punishment from the schools. So far our Authority has not made up its mind, and I think it is up to us as Governors to make our views known on the subject. I don't think this should take up much of our time because, no doubt, we are all agreed that physical violence against a child is repulsive and should, justifiably, be banned from schools.'

Major Darnall: 'Well, it depends what you mean by physical violence. I'm certainly against making an official caning of a child – you know – all that business about having to have a witness and recording the caning in the punishment book – but there's nothing wrong in thumping a kid on the spot when he's done something wrong. I can tell you, some of 'em need it.'

Ms Fang: '*Thumping a kid!* . . . You mean you approve of a person weighing twelve stone physically attacking a person weighing three stone?'

Major Darnall: 'Now you're talking rubbish; I'm talking about a quick flip around the ear when necessary. Good God above, I had a few whacks in my time and it certainly did me no harm.'

Mr Dyer: 'But we hope things have improved a little since your time, Major . . .'

Ms Fang: 'How can we expect to prevent violence in society when we permit violence against children in our schools?'

Mrs Richardson: 'I'm sure you're really exaggerating it all. Children *do* need a slap sometimes and I, as a parent, am quite happy to leave it to the discretion and good sense of the staff at St. Claude's to decide when some form of chastisement is necessary.'

(This liberal attitude is typical of a nice person like Mrs Richardson who has two nice little girls like Felicity and Venetia who will work their way through school quietly and conscientiously without requiring a raised voice, never mind a raised hand. But someone like Mrs Hulbert would come roaring into school with a clenched fist if any member of staff so much as prodded either Ricky or Darren.)

Mrs Glugburn: 'Before we all get bogged down on this, let us have Mr Masterton's opinion. After all, he has to personally deal with this problem.'

(I was waiting for this one – and wondered how Mr Masterton would cope with it. A gentle man himself, I have never known him do more than slightly shove a naughty child, but we both knew that Miss Krantz slaps the calves of recalcitrant children in her class and also that Mr Singleton keeps a long bamboo cane. Mr Singleton has never, to my knowledge, struck a child with his cane, but he uses it to remarkable effect upon their desks. A very skilful cane manipulator, he brings it down with an impressive thwack across the desk and within a fraction of an inch of the hands of any child who is messing about.)

Mr Masterton (mildly): 'Well, the question doesn't arise really; we don't have any problems with discipline at St. Claude's.'

Mr Dyer: 'Nevertheless, I do feel that we, as Governors of St. Claude's, should put our joint views in writing and place a document before The Authority.'

(Sorting out the exact wording of the proposed statement to The Authority takes nearly half an hour. We end up with the sentence: 'The Governors of St. Claude's are totally opposed to the use of corporal punishment in schools, but accept that certain circumstances may arise in which a teacher may find himself or herself obliged to take some form of appropriate action' . . . and Mrs Glugburn agrees to write the letter.)

Mrs Glugburn: 'Well, if that concludes Any Other Business I will now declare the . . .'

Ms Fang: 'Before we finish there is a point I would like to bring up. It has particular relevance to St. Claude's because of the fair proportion of coloured children we have. As you know, under Section II of the Government Aid for Ethnic Minorities Act, all local authorities are entitled to claim help from central funds to aid the problems of the inner-city area. I feel very strongly that our Authority is dragging its feet here and not claiming a full entitlement, and so I propose . . .'

(Miss Krantz sighs heavily and looks at her watch; Major

121

Darnall shuffles his papers into a neat pile, clicks his ballpoint pen into the 'off' position and puts it into his pocket. Mrs Richardson begins to sag in her chair. Mrs Glugburn folds her arms and stares hard at Ms Fang.)

Ms Fang: '. . . that we send the following statement to The Authority: "We, the Governors of St. Claude's, whilst accepting that all inner-city needs have to be determined in a context of continuous dialogue and competing demands, feel that on the question of Section II, the Authority should constantly review its requirements and this should include regularly looking at ways of maximizing the amount of resource input it can achieve from all sources, including Section II."'

Me: 'Pardon?'

(Ms Fang repeats her statement, and then hands to me the piece of paper from which she was reading. Nobody argues. The proposal is seconded by Mr Pugh, and a motion is carried. Mrs Glugburn agrees to write the letter – and I attach Ms Fang's statement to my notes . . . and I'm still wondering what it means.)

*　　　*　　　*

Sometimes now the Governors' Meetings go on for so long that we are unable to get through all the business, and an extra meeting is called during the same term. But one thing is quite clear to me. Although our new Governors appear to be sincerely interested in education, they are not the least bit interested in St. Claude's. They all seem to be involved in committee work in various parts of the city, and there is much consulting of diaries and notebooks before we can ever decide upon the date of the next meeting. They are all far too busy to come to our Concerts, Sports Day, or Fayre Days, and I don't think any of them has ever spoken more than one or two words to the children. Fortunately, we still have Major Darnall to act as Father Christmas each year, and Mrs Glugburn to occupy the seat of honour at our concerts. Mr Derby still slips in every now and then to see Mr Masterton and to present the school with some books, and every term a group of Mr Appleby's children pay a visit to old Mrs Bennett. Mr Bender, I'm afraid, has taken the huff since losing his place on our Governing

Body. We now have to pay for the hire of his coaches.

I was recently chatting to Miss Krantz about the role of the school governor today and I said that I thought a governing body was now an anachronism; that there certainly had been some point in such a body in the days when the local squire and vicar kept a benevolently patronising eye upon the local Board School, but that those days were now over and today it served no useful purpose. She didn't agree with me and pointed out that if it hadn't been for Mrs Glugburn, for example, the local community would never have been granted the services of the Lollipop Lady who shepherds the children across the main road at the bottom of the hill. Miss Krantz also reminded me that all school teachers are selected by the school governors. I didn't argue with Miss Krantz, (it is pointless arguing with Miss Krantz) but I can see several flaws in the points she makes. I agree that we owe our Lollipop Lady to Mrs Glugburn. But this came about because Mrs Glugburn is Mrs Glugburn – not because she is a school governor, and although the school governors interviewing a prospective member of staff may *feel* they are playing a power game it is, in fact, an illusion. School governors can certainly *recommend* a staff appointment. They can't *make* it.

Let us assume, for example, that a collection of school governors of a certain political persuasion wished to ensure that the teacher appointed to a vacant post at the school shared their views. If the Headteacher also shared their views then, provided that the applicant appeared also to be a good teacher, the appointment might be made. (*No* Headteacher, no matter how politically-minded, is going to appoint a teacher who seems to be useless.) But if the Headteacher didn't like the applicant then, no matter how many governors voted against him, all he has to do is to inform the Local Authority of his doubts and they will, if they share his concern, exercise their right of veto. The appointment will not be made – without any explanation necessarily having to be given.

The same rules apply even more emphatically when the appointment has to be made of a Headteacher. On these occasions all applications for the vacant post have, first of all, to be submitted to the Local Authority – who will then draw up a short list of applicants whose letters of application will be forwarded to the Chairman of Governors. So far as The Authority is concerned the matter is, from then on, unimportant. They have made sure that all the 'approved' applicants are worthy of the appointment, so far as they are concerned. It doesn't matter which one is appointed – they all suit the pattern of acceptability demanded by The Authority. The Governors can amuse themselves for as long as they like choosing between these applicants but – just to make sure that nothing goes amiss – one of the Authority's Advisers will *always* sit in at these interviews.

The Authority believes in keeping an eye upon the current plans of school governors, and it insists that two copies of all documents for their termly meetings (including Minutes and Agenda) are sent to the Chief Education Officer in advance of each meeting – and the Chief Education Officer can ask one of his Advisers to drop in on any of these meetings, without warning, if he thinks it is desirable.

But although, on the face of it, school governors appear to have outlived their original purpose, they seem to have acquired a new one in that a school governing body serves as a harmless emotional outlet for the frustrations of angry teachers, parents and members of the local community, and there is every indication that the Local Authority – recognising the value of such an outlet – is giving school governors much encouragement. On any educational matter of national interest the 'views' of the governors are sought, and sometimes Governors Dyer, Pugh and Fang have found themselves without time to raise matters under Any Other Business because of some document or other I have been asked to put before the meeting. Every term I will receive one or two such documents – each running to a dozen or more closely-typed pages of A4 paper. Last year, for example, at the request of The Authority, we discussed sections of the Plowden Report – the Nuffield Foundation Resources for Learning Project – Health & Safety (First Aid in Schools) Regulations 1981 – the working paper on The School Curriculum – and the Department of Education & Science Report 'Teacher Training and Preparation for Working Life'. Deliberation of these papers necessitated many hours of meeting time and many long letters which Mrs Glugburn composed and I typed.

So, on the whole, I think that we at St. Claude's need have no worries about the 'Red Threat to our Schools'. We shall carry on writing long letters to The Authority; we shall reply to all their requests for our views – and we shall also give our unasked-for opinions on matters like the Admission of Rising Fives – the Proposed new Letting Procedures of School Premises – and the new Planned Admission Levels. We shall continue pressing our demands for attention to leaking roofs, unpainted corridors, and the inadequate heating system. We shall ask for consideration to be given to the provision of extra staff toilet accommodation and some form of staff car-parking facility. We shall protest strongly about our overcrowded classrooms, the rise in the price of school meals, and the inadequately ventilated boys' toilets. We shall press all our claims vigorously, persistently and with unwavering determination. And nothing will happen.

CHAPTER EIGHT

Children's Health

To cope with the day-to-day minor accidents and ailments at St. Claude's I have a First Aid cupboard which contains cotton wool, sticking plasters, bandages, antiseptic cream and lotions, safety pins, a thermometer, an eye bath and a wasp-sting aerosol. There are also two large bottles of aspirin and paracetamol for the staff. For the children who are 'not feeling very well' there is a dingy cubicle called the Medical Room (which contains one hard chair, a gas fire, a horse-hair examination couch and several army-type blankets) where they are sent to lie down. A child sent to the Medical Room will be accompanied by a classmate who will keep an eye on him or her, and will offer comfort in the way of answering requests for glasses of water or a book from the school library. As the Medical Room is right next door to the office it frequently happens that the sounds of laughter and larking about the other side of my wall will indicate to me that the child 'not feeling very well' is obviously now 'feeling much better', and I go in and dispatch them both back to class. But sometimes a child's flushed face and miserable expression will show all too clearly that the child is ill and should not be at school.

Working mothers of primary school aged children must sometimes have very difficult decisions to make. When faced with a complaining child first thing in the morning a mother with a job to go to has to ask herself – is my child *so* bad that I should risk my employer's wrath by staying home, or is this ailment something that will pass off, or is the child just putting it on? Caring mothers faced with this dilemma will sometimes bring the child to school and then come and see me in the office . . . 'John said he had an awful tummy ache this morning, but I thought I'd bring him to school as it might just pass off; but if he continues to grizzle about it please let me know . . . you can get hold of me at this telephone number . . .' Uncaring mothers just push the complaining offspring through the door and make off. And I try to settle the child down as comfortably as possible between the army blankets upon the horse-hair examination couch.

Some of our children have disabilities which don't prevent them coming to school but which present them (and me) with a few problems. We have a little epileptic girl who has a fit nearly every week and also wets her knickers every day and for whom I keep a spare set of knickers, skirts and socks in my First Aid cupboard. We have two spastic boys who have frequent tumbles, the results of which need patching up, and one little girl with chronic asthma. The other children seem to accept these disabilities with kindliness and aplomb. Neither of the spastic boys has ever been attacked or even pushed around by any of our toughie juniors, and Susan, the little girl with asthma, is always accompanied by a caring group of her female peers who attend to her every whim. Susan has tablets and an inhaler which I keep in the office, but she never has to come for them by herself. Almost daily a little posse of girls from her class will come to the office because 'Susan needs her whezy sniffer'. The convulsions of epileptic Angela are observed with curiosity. 'What do *you* want?' I said crossly the other day to Jason Spragg who had come into the office. '*I* don't want anything. I just thought you ought to know that Angela is having a fit in the playground.' (I later gathered that Jason's motives for conveying this news to the office were not so much his concern for the writhing Angela but irritation that the crowd of interested onlookers was interrupting the game of football.)

Injuries fascinate the children – especially the girls. Any child who has a bleeding knee, a grazed elbow, a squeezed finger or a bumped head will be accompanied to the office by four or five children who, if I am not there to prevent them, will dive into the First Aid cupboard and pull out

127

plasters, bandages and cream – and fight amongst themselves trying to decide how the job should be done and who is going to do it. I once returned to the office to find a slightly tearful but rather bemused Darren Hulbert sitting on a chair with his outstretched leg being supported by his brother. One little girl held Darren's hand, another was stroking his forehead saying 'There, there!' whilst two others (one wielding a wet paper towel and the other squeezing out inches of antiseptic cream) were arguing the relative merits of 'washing first' or applying 'disinfectant' to a knee which appeared to be covered more in dirt than blood. When I am there to take charge of an injured child, his attendants will stand by and watch with riveted concentration and bated breath whilst I investigate a wound and decide what to do. I am given plenty of advice. 'He'll need a bandage for that; a plaster won't stay on' . . . 'That's an old scab he's been picking; that's why it's bleeding so much' . . . 'That stuff in the bottle stings mind' . . . 'If you keep picking a scab you bleed to death don't you?' Willing helpers will dash off to moisten cotton wool; willing fingers will help tie a bandage, or press down the edges of a plaster, or hold aside blood-matted hair . . . 'Gosh, you ought to see this hole in your head . . . it's *huge*!'

But whilst most of the children respond sympathetically to the accidents of others, they can't always judge the seriousness of a situation. An infant once came rushing into my office; her little white face was round-eyed with horror and she was almost speechless. When she eventually found the words she blurted out, 'Jamie Brown's Mummy has fallen down the stairs and her head's come off!' Remembering that the newly-installed Fire Door with its cruelly strong glass was situated at the bottom of the stairs, I tore from the office expecting to be confronted by the appalling spectacle of a decapitated Mrs Brown in a bloody huddle athwart a broken pane . . . only to find the embarrassed lady on her hands and knees grovelling beneath the stationery cupboard to retrieve her wig. On another occasion I was busily typing when a small movement in the corner of the room caught my eye and there, at the First Aid cupboard, was a junior girl helping herself to a plaster. Having given the child a one-minute lecture upon the wrongness of her action, I then asked her what she wanted the plaster for. 'Tanya,' was the answer.

'Why does Tanya want a plaster?'

'She's cut her face.'

'Then ask Tanya to come to the office.'

'She can't.'

'Why not?'

'She's lying in the playground; I think she's fainted.'

Tanya, lying unconscious at the base of the climbing frame, was later found to have a fractured skull and was in hospital for several months.

Tanya's accident was one of those occasions when I dialled 999. I send for one of the emergency services (usually the ambulance service, but sometimes the Fire Brigade) on average, I should think, once a term. I know of some schools where such freedom of action is not permitted the secretary. Before 999 is dialled the Head must be consulted or, in the Head's absence, the Deputy Head. If the Head is away on a Course (and many of them often are) and, say, the Deputy Head has gone to the games field, many valuable minutes must be lost whilst the decision is made as to who is in charge and what must be done in the circumstances. Fortunately, at St. Claude's, there are no such foolish strictures. If a situation crops up that I think cannot be handled by anyone in the school I dial 999 – and have always received a first-class response from the emergency service called. Naturally, there have been a few false alarms (like the time a careless painting contractor set fire to an old window frame with his blow torch but managed to put out the fire before the Brigade arrived . . . and the time a child, apparently choking to death with a pencil rubber stuck in its windpipe, suddenly coughed – gulped – and then said normally, 'It's all right; I've just swallowed it,') but the unnecessarily summoned emergency men never mind. Perhaps they feel that the maxim 'better safe than sorry' is especially relevant to a primary school. I know that I do.

With the school equipped to look after everyday mishaps and a Local Authority health scheme which watches over the children throughout their school life we would seem to have, on the face of it, an ideal system for the maintenance of children's health. When a new child arrives at St. Claude's, I enter its name in our Register and notify all the various departments in The Authority's Child Health Service. The child's name will then be slotted into a system which provides for frequent checks upon eyes, teeth, ears, weight and general health. Once a term, at each school, there will be a Medical Inspection attended by The Authority's current Child Health Doctor, and any new children at the school will automatically have their names put down for the first available Medical Inspection. If the child is found to be fit and healthy it will not be put forward for a further full medical inspection whilst at primary school – unless a specific request comes from the Headteacher or parent. If, on the other hand, some defect is found, then helpful measures will be suggested to the parent, and the child will be asked to attend further medical inspections at regular intervals throughout its school life. But a child cannot be examined by the school doctor without the written permission of the parent . . . and this is where the scheme falls down.

Each term, when I receive from The Authority notification of the next Medical Inspection and the names of the children booked for it, I send out letters to the parents concerned giving them the date and time of the appointment – inviting them to attend if they wish – asking them to sign giving permission for the examination to take place without them if they can't come – and asking them to give certain items of information regarding any chronic illnesses and any inoculations the child may have had. Responsible and caring parents return the form, duly completed, and giving their permission without hesitation. Irresponsible and uncaring parents lose the form and forget the date. But the children of responsible and caring parents are usually under the regular care of the family doctor anyway, and don't *need* The Authority's health service; whereas the children with perpetual cold sores, lank dirty hair, lack-lustre eyes or flea-bitten legs often have parents who can't be bothered to take their child to the family doctor, let alone go to the trouble of co-operating with the school health scheme. When such a child misses several successive Medical Inspections a 'home visit' will be made by the local Health Visitor with the purpose of persuading mother to take the child to the Clinic. But if no-one is at home (or will come to the door) then many weeks may pass before a busy Health Visitor can finally pin down mother who will, more often than not, agree with everything said to her . . . and then dismiss it all from her mind as soon as the Visitor has gone.

If it is suspected that a child is ill-treated or neglected at home to such an extent that action should be taken to remove the child to 'a place of safety', then of course there are legal measures open to the school – and if a child came to school battered and injured then obviously no-one would hesitate to use these powers. But it's not the viciously battered children I'm thinking of – it's the pathetic little things who creep through their school days undernourished and unkempt; neglected, yes – but not to such an extent that they should be taken away from their parent(s). Or should they? Who is going to make the decision?

I can remember one tired-looking, pale-faced little boy who went through both infant classes without attending a Medical Inspection because parental permission was never forthcoming, and the parents were never available for a 'home visit'. He was frequently absent from school, because of sickness, but as both parents were doctors (father an orthopaedic consultant, and mother in general practice) no particular concern was felt as it was presumed that the parents knew what they were doing. He was academically far behind the rest of his class; he was uncommunicative and always preferred to play by himself. We all thought that he was very dull, almost to the point of qualifying for ESN (Educationally Sub-Normal) classification, until the day when, by chance, he was tested by the visiting audiometrician on her annual visit. She discovered that the child was almost stone deaf in both ears.

The Audiometrician, Dentist and School Nurse all make regular visits to the school, and they can examine the children without getting prior permission from the parents. Parents *do* have rights in this matter of course – but any parent who objects to The Authority's health officers laying hands on their child will have to write to the school expressly forbidding it; otherwise the benevolent net of Health Care will submit the child to being weighed, measured and having its eyes, teeth and ears looked at.

(Whilst it is accepted that parents *should* have this right – and a few of our commune dwellers exercise it – it is a little frustrating when an outbreak of head lice in a particular class is suspected to have stemmed from a bushy-haired pupil who is forbidden by its mother to co-operate in the general 'head-hunt' that traditionally takes place on these occasions.)

The Audiometrician comes once a year to test all the 'new' children who have come to the school since her last visit. She is a pleasant lady with a fascinating box of highly complex electronic equipment which the children regard as a new sort of audio-video game . . . 'Now just put on these headphones, dear, and when you hear a tiny noise you press that button and see what a pretty light comes on. The system, albeit 100% electronically efficient, has its limitations. Children who want to see the pretty light just press the button anyway, and children who want to do what they think is required of them will press it even when they can't hear anything. But if the Audiometrician suspects that a child hasn't given an honest response she will go back to the old fashioned turn-your-back-and-say-when-you-can-hear-me-bang-on-this-drum method. Any child whose hearing appears to be normal will not be tested again whilst at school. Any child about whom there are doubts will be referred to the Hearing Clinic for a full test. I don't know what happens at the Hearing Clinic but, once again, it depends upon co-operative parents to actually take the child there.

When the School Dentists come we have to be highly organised to receive them. A team of them will set up in the rather cramped conditions of the Medical Room and I will arrange for every child in the school – six of them at a time – to visit the Medical Room, each one clutching his or her medical card. Any child whose teeth appear to need some attention will be given a note to take home. This note invites the parent to take the child to the dental hospital, or to their own dentist. Some of the notes get home; some of the parents take appropriate action.

The most frequent Health Authority visitor to the school is, of course, our School Nurse. She comes regularly every week and systematically goes through each class of children, testing their eyes, weighing them, measuring them and noting their general health. Nurse seems to operate as a free agent – making appointments for children at the eye hospital – visiting parents to talk about problems of weight or bad skin – contacting the various Welfare Agencies if she is worried about a particular family and, of course, putting forward children's names for the next Medical Inspection. Nurse has been with us for many years and knows all the children, their parents and the staff. We are all very fond of her and will be sorry when she retires next year. Nurse, however, will not be sorry. Although she says she will miss coming to visit her schools, she is finding it all a bit too much these days, and the St. Claude's children are particularly trying. A very gentle, soft-spoken and rather dithery person, she has great difficulty in controlling the juniors, who play jokes upon her without mercy. She told me a few weeks ago that she would have to test the eyes of Mr Appleby's class all over again because someone had muddled up her cards. 'I had the children in line, and the cards in a pile in the correct order. Someone must have shuffled the cards whilst I was making sure a child had its eye covered correctly; it wasn't until I found myself writing a boy's eyesight on a girl's card that I realised what had happened.' To add to her burden of work that day someone had let down the tyres of her bicycle and had hidden her pump.

But I think that naughty children are the least of Nurse's worries. She is under extra pressure these days because of a reorganisation currently taking place within the Health Authority; boundaries are being changed and work patterns altered. She is losing schools she enjoys visiting and is having to take on others that are distant and unknown. But her biggest headache is the change in the system of recording pupils' details. I found her in the staffroom the other day looking very worried and surrounded by medical record cards. She was battling with the task of transferring information from the old cards to the new – and when she showed me one of the new cards I began to grasp the extent of her difficulties.

Whereas on the old card she just filled in the child's name, address and age at the top, and there was plenty of blank space in which to record the child's weight, height and eyesight, together with useful little comments like 'A good strong healthy boy', or 'Rather thin and smells of urine' . . . now she has to complete little boxes headed 'height percentile; height vel cm/yr. weight kg/lb; bone maturity score and skeletal age' – which neither she nor I understand. Moreover the age has to be 'decimalised'. In order to help her 'decimalise' the child's age there is given on each card a table (which makes no allowance, I notice, for leap year) which explains that each date in the calendar is marked in terms of thousandths of the year. Thus 7th Jan. 1962 would be 62.016. The age of a child at examination would then be obtained (the chart claims) by a simple subtraction. E.g. 62.016–59.474=2.542 . . . and the last figure is 'rounded off' (whatever that means). Having decimalised the child's age, and obtained its height vel. cm/yr. weight kg/lb and bone maturity score – you then plot these details on a chart which (according to the author of the new card) will 'greatly facilitate the computing of velocity'.

But the thing about this new card that intrigues me is the extra information demanded. The boys must have their genital (penis) development recorded, together with testes (vol. in ml) and scrotal skin (colour); the girls must be measured for breast development (including projection of areola and papilla); and both must submit to an examination of colour and density of pubic hair. (Nurse is helped in her measurement of testes by the information given on the card that 'testes sizes are judged by comparison with the Prader Orchidometer – Zachmann, Prader, Kind, Haffinger & Budliger, Helv. Paed. Acta. 29, 61-72 1974'.) These new cards will accompany the child through primary school and secondary school. The chart is made out in ages from 0-19 years. I'm not sure how the nurse comes to grips with the pre-school vital statistics of a 0-year-old child, and the mind boggles at the thought of, say, a 25-year-old school nurse attempting to measure the length of the penis of a strapping, virile 19-year-old 6th form scholar. I mean to say, at which stage does she . . . well, what I mean is – what if . . . well. Good Heavens above. No wonder our nurse is looking forward to retirement.

The Educational Psychologist (whose work seems to straddle the Health Service and the Education Service) visits schools only at the request of the Headteacher. Our Educational Psychologist is an earnest young lady with long dark hair and thick glasses. She usually comes to the school wearing a shabby dirndl skirt with an uneven hem, an old goatskin jacket, and wrinkled coloured tights. She carries a battered leather case which contains her 'equipment' and she talks in a low mutter which makes her an embarrassing person to sit next to during coffee break in the staffroom. The Educational Psychologist is usually called to the school when it is felt that a child who is not doing very well academically (or who is behaving appallingly) may have deep psychological problems which, if identified, can be sorted out. A child so singled out for psychological attention will sit with the Educational Psychologist in the library, and will be asked to answer questions, play pencil and paper games, draw pictures, and move around various coloured plastic shapes. This interview, can, of course, only take place with the parent's permission and the child's co-operation. If both are forthcoming, then the Educational Psychologist will carry out her tests and make a lot of notes which will eventually appear in the form of a letter of advice to the Headteacher.

Last year, however, we had a flurry of visits from the Educational Psychologist for a different reason. Mrs Harrowes (one of our more ambitious mothers) whose pleasant and normal little girl Amelia was in the 4th year juniors, felt that her child was 'under functioning' (her expression, not mine), because she was not sufficiently stretched academically. She asked if the Educational Psychologist would carry out an I.Q. test on the child. Mr Masterton agreed – the Educational Psychologist came – and produced an I.Q. figure for Amelia which astonished Mr Masterton, delighted Mrs Harrowes, but infuriated several other mothers (to whom Mrs Harrowes boasted) each of whom felt that *her* child could knock spots off Amelia Harrowes. The requests for examination of 'under functioning' juniors came in thick and fast and our co-operative Educational Psychologist came to St. Claude's several times during one fortnight to carry out the tests. Mr Masterton, who was now beginning to regret the whole thing, didn't know whether to be relieved or worried when the Educational Psychologist produced a further set of very high I.Q.s. The group of mothers concerned (five in all) were not prepared to let the matter rest. What did Mr Masterton intend doing about these very bright children who were being 'let down' by the education system at St. Claude's?

By making enquiries of The Society for Gifted Children, Mr Masterton discovered that a teacher who had been specially trained to cope with the Gifted Child was currently working at St. Jude's School, just across the river from us. Arrangements were made for our five children (two boys and three girls) to go across to St. Jude's for two sessions of mind-extending education per week. The whole thing was a bit of a nuisance (someone had to take them there and bring them back and, although all the mums involved promised to help with transport, it usually fell to Mr Appleby or Mr Masterton to do the to-ing and fro-ing) but fortunately it didn't last very long. One by one the mums started to go off the idea when it was discovered that the specially trained teacher at St. Jude's was, when not taking the Gifted Children, carrying on with her normal duties as Remedial Teacher – coping with the Maladjusted, Educationally Sub-Normal, and disruptive children from the surrounding schools. One by one the children were withdrawn from the Gifted Children class until only Amelia Harrowes was left. She finally rebelled and refused to go – and the whole thing fizzled out.

The Educational Psychologist had seen these five children at the request of parents who were very articulate and *positive* people, and as the final report on each child was short, pleasing and intelligible, Mr Masterton let each mother see the Psychologist's comment on her child. But this is not generally the case at St. Claude's. Usually the child interviewed is allegedly disturbed or repressed in some way, and the Educational Psychologist's report is long. Very long. It is not meant to be seen by the parent and is usually couched in terms which baffle the uninformed. Take the report on Marlene Coggins, for example. When Marlene went through a phase of refusing to work at all and, instead of doing her 'number work' doodled all over her exercise book drawing naked ladies with grossly large breasts, Mr Masterton felt the time had come to call for advice from the Educational Psychologist. Mrs Coggins readily agreed and Marlene spent about an hour in the library one afternoon going through the routine of answering questions, doodling to order, and playing with plastic cubes and triangles.

The report, when it arrived a fortnight later, ran to two pages of A4 typing and went something like this:

To: H. Masterton Esq., B.A., From: Education Dept., Head of St. Claude's School   Child Guidance Clinic.
        re: Marlene Coggins (10 years 3 months).

Further to my recent examination of Marlene I must say, initially, that she certainly related well and obtained Verbal I.Q. 113 on the W.I.S.C., with performance at 94 and full scale 104. I detected a certain behavioural sub-nominal impulsisation on her motility development, and there was definite negative input on the related impressional patterns of interaction. However, her sub-test scores were as follows: Comprehension 10, Arithmetic 12, Similarities 12, Digit Span 14, Audition Association 34, and Grammatic Closure 49. There was good attention potential and immediate memory score. I am a little concerned at her unaligned accountability to the response conception. Could she be suffering from some sort of 'weltangst' towards her peers? Equally, her mother's own irregular domestic arrangement probably has some bearing upon the amplifiable causality of the semantic differential that I observed. On the other hand her drawing of a man was very detailed and included hairy arms and legs as well as toes (4 on each foot) and with the correct number of fingers. (Block design and object assembly were 7 and 8 respectively – and coding was 9.) She scored (Good enough) at 9.25. I took the opportunity of doing some data-based problematic sampling upon these results – and my findings were most interesting . . .' etc. etc.

The report ended with the sentence: 'I hope these comments will be of help to you.'

CHAPTER NINE

Alarms and Disorders

The front door and the playground gates of St. Claude's are unlocked by Mr Potts at about 8 o'clock in the morning, and they are locked again in the early evening after the school has been cleaned, unless there is an evening 'letting' – in which case it could be nearly midnight before the school is made secure again. During all these open hours (and especially during the school day) many people pass through the gates and doors; not only children and parents, but also students, officials from The Authority, men wanting to deliver things or mend things or read the meters, and other visitors. Not all of the visitors have benevolent intentions. A few years ago someone walked into the school one morning when all the children and teachers were gathered in the hall for morning Assembly, and when I was in the office sorting out the dinner registers. This person went into the staffroom (which is clearly labelled) where Mrs Snow and Miss Krantz had left their handbags, and where Mr Appleby had left his jacket over the back of a chair. It was immediately after Assembly that Mr Appleby retrieved his jacket and discovered that his wallet had gone. Both ladies instantly checked their handbags and found that their purses were missing. I contacted the police and a detective came to see us, but he wasn't at all hopeful. 'There have been a lot of walk-in thefts in schools in this area recently,' he said, 'and it usually happens during Assembly time.' But a short while later we had a lunchtime intruder who, finding the office empty, helped himself/herself to all the pound notes in the school fund tin – which I had foolishly left in an unlocked drawer in my desk.

The ease with which people walk into schools and wander around unchallenged can be explained. Only the Headteacher, the secretary or the caretaker feel it is their duty to find out who unknown visitors are. If the Headteacher happens to be absent, the secretary away at the post office, and the caretaker off duty, any teacher foolish enough to approach a stranger and ask what he wants may find himself trying to sort out the problems of an electrician who wants to get into the swimming pool, but finds that it is locked and no-one knows where the key is; or a man from the museum who has come to collect several exhibits due for return and no-one knows who borrowed them or where they might be found; or a man, with a pane of glass under his arm, who wants to borrow the caretaker's ladder to reach the broken library window but no-one knows where the caretaker keeps the ladder. The bona fide visitor will stand patiently in the office waiting for someone to *do something* to help. This is why most teachers (when nipping out of class to go to the toilet, or on their way to the staffroom to enjoy a smoke or a cup of coffee) will walk quickly past a wandering stranger in the corridor with a bright smile and a nod. If he stops to ask 'Can I help you?' he may find himself lumbered.

(I understand that 'walk-in' thefts are an even bigger problem at secondary schools, where the number of strangers milling about the place must amount to dozens daily. I know of one secondary school where the entire stock of sewing machines was removed from a classroom one lunchtime. Presumably if the people loading the sewing machines into their van were challenged by a teacher – a *most* unlikely event at secondary school I believe – the teacher would have been informed that the machines were 'going for servicing'; an explanation which would not have been queried.)

Maintaining security in the school office can sometimes put me in an embarrassing position. Since the theft of that money from my drawer I have never been daft enough to leave the office (even just for a few minutes) without locking away all loose money. But if a visitor comes into the office when I am actually counting out and bagging-up the dinner money ready for banking – and the purpose of the visitor involves me leaving the office – what do I do about all the money on my desk? There is no problem if the visitor is a man who has come to mend the fence or measure up the playground or somesuch. I simply accompany the man from the office and, locking the door behind me, give him a knowing smile and make some comment about 'can't be too careful – never know who might come in' – and then I take him to wherever he wants to go. The embarrassing visitor is the one who comes in and asks for Mr Masterton . . . and I know that Mr Masterton is the other side of the school pinning up notices, or checking through the library stocks. Do I gather up all the money and take it with me? Or do I leave the office and trust to the honesty of the person waiting there? I usually get around this by giving the visitor a cheerful smile and saying something like 'Oh, he's in the Assembly Hall putting up pictures – perhaps you'd like to wander across and find him.'

This matey go-and-help-yourself attitude has earned me a few odd looks from time to time, but casual callers who have come, say, to try and sell him books — or friendly mums who want to talk to him about their child – usually co-operate and go on a headmaster hunt. But one large and important-looking lady who once visited when I was involved in my weekly count-up refused to budge. 'I am the Senior Adviser for Infant Education,' she informed me, 'Mr Masterton is expecting me; perhaps you will kindly tell him that I am here.' I hesitated. The lady *might* be telling the truth. (She was.) But on the other hand she might be light-fingered and Up to No Good – and there was about £150 in piles of notes and assorted coins upon my desk. I carefully gathered it all together, putting elastic bands around the notes and scooping the loose coins into a large bank bag. I took it across the room to the metal filing cabinet; locked it inside, and left the room taking the key with me. I walked several yards down the corridor to the staffroom (where Mr Masterton was trying to put a new plug on the electric kettle) and returned with him to the office. I suppose I was away from my desk for about 30 seconds. I avoided the lady's eyes as I crossed the office and unlocked my filing cabinet again, but I could see that her face was bright red.

From time to time the children steal money and small articles from each other – and from the teacher's desk drawer. All primary school teachers' desk drawers contain assorted bits of paper, sheets of card, registers, crayons, ballpoint pens, chalk, Sellotape, scissors, elastic bands, a staple gun, Bluetack adhesive, string, dice, odd plastic counters and bits of Lego, confiscated comics and chewing gum, a broken stop watch, one or two tape cassettes and a few small tins with money in. (If you don't believe me, ask to look inside the drawer of *your* child's teacher. If the drawer can be opened fully – an unlikely event because of all the paper jammed down the back – you will find most, if not all, of the before-mentioned articles.) And the children, of course, find these drawers fascinating.

Bearing in mind that most children are thieving little animals by instinct (well, I bear it in mind, even if you don't) we get surprisingly little trouble at St. Claude's. Children who haven't been taught that it is *wrong* to steal usually reveal themselves in Mrs Snow's class – either because they are caught stealing someone else's bar of chocolate or packet of crisps or, more usually, because they help themselves to some of the dinner money whilst the dinner money tin is in their hands on its way from the classroom to the office. The fact that you can't get away with stealing dinner money is one of the first lessons of life that these children learn. If the money in the tin doesn't equal the money written in the register I am in that classroom almost on the heels of the child who brought me the tin and register. The shock of being caught so quickly at stealing the dinner money has a chastening effect on some infants – and they probably won't steal again. Others just learn to be more crafty.

Some children steal persistently, and can't seem to help it. Sharon Parsons for example. She stole dinner money when she was in Mrs Snow's class (and was cunning enough not to keep the money in her possession, but to hide it in a crack in the playground wall whilst on her way from classroom to office), and she also once stole a £10 note from Mrs Snow's handbag. This last crime came to light when one of Mrs Snow's infants went up to her in the middle of the morning and told her that there was a purse in one of the lavatories. Mrs Snow went to investigate, and

141

found the purse to be her own. The sodden purse still contained Mrs Snow's front door key and some loose change, but a £10 note was missing. The children were questioned and all asked to turn out their lockers, but the culprit was not discovered until the following day. I happened to call in the local newsagent's shop for my morning paper and the proprietor took me aside. 'A little girl changed a £10 note in here yesterday and bought a whole load of sweets and chocolate. Seemed a bit fishy to me.' The description was that of Sharon. When Mrs Snow looked in Sharon's locker she found it filled with packets of sweets, bars of chocolate – and about £7.20 in cash.

Sweets have always been Sharon's undoing, it seems. Her mother now has to pay for Sharon's dinners by cheque because Sharon can't be trusted to walk past the newsagent's shop carrying her dinner money. She steals sweets from the pockets of other children, and once she was caught opening up the lunch boxes in the cloakroom and taking out any bars of chocolate she found.

Sharon is adopted. Her parents, who own a bistro and pizza bar in the centre of the city, have two other children (of their own) and Sharon was adopted because Mrs Parsons always wanted three children . . . 'and after I'd had my hysterectomy we decided to *adopt*.' Sharon (half Italian) is a very pretty child and at one time all three of Mrs Parsons' daughters were in school together. But the elder girls, who are twins, were taken away from St. Claude's when they reached the first-year junior stage and were sent to a private preparatory school. All three children appear well-dressed and cared for – but it was noticeable that Sharon's clothes, although neat and tidy, were much cheaper than those of her elder sisters. Sharon, now in Mr Singleton's class, will undoubtedly be with us until the end of her primary education, and will probably pass on to the local secondary school.

Sharon's problems (which are also a problem to us and the children who are unfortunate enough to sit next to her, or hang their coats next to hers) have turned her into a rather lonely, unsociable child. She is by no means stupid. It can only be hoped that thieving is something she will grow out of as she matures. (Before long I can see someone suggesting that Sharon has a session with pencil, paper and plastic shapes in the library with the Educational Psychologist, who will probably advise us that '. . . Sharon has a low attention threshold, and these disturbing elements in her behaviour should be seen as cyclical and not linear because their evaluation must be seen against the background of the recurring cycle of imagined deprivation in Sharon's relationship with her adoptive parents.')

Mr Ball, who keeps the newsagent-cum-sweet shop near the school, used to complain a lot about the St. Claude's children and their shoplifting habits. As his attractive displays of Toffee Chews, Licorice Dips, Fruity Gobstoppers and Chocolate Crunchies are all within infant reaching height I was not at all surprised that he gets trouble – and I told him so. He was quite huffy about this, and reckoned that we at St. Claude's were failing in our duty to teach the children decent standards of behaviour. 'I couldn't possibly make it all secure against your thieving lot,' he said. 'This place is like Piccadilly Circus first thing in the morning . . . I can't keep my eyes on what they are doing at all the display stands.'

Having put up with Mr Ball's complaints for a long time, Mr Masterton decided to take firm action. The newsagent's shop was put out of bounds to all St. Claude's children, and he formed a rota of responsible junior girls to stand outside the shop during the lunch period to turn away any of our children who were hovering nearby. I kept a check on the shop first thing in the morning just before school opened, and Mr Masterton stood in the shop doorway for ten minutes after school had closed. With no St. Claude's children in the shop before school each day, it certainly didn't look like Piccadilly Circus in there. Mr Ball appeared to be selling only newspapers. We kept this up for a week – and then relented. I don't know whether our children have stopped stealing from Mr Ball – but he has certainly stopped complaining.

When our junior boys leave us for secondary school a few of them will always return the following autumn – after dark. They usually break in through the Medical Room window (it is commonly known that this is the easiest way to get into the school) but they don't often get much further because Mr Potts locks all doors throughout the school; a

143

fact which most children wouldn't realise – and they don't come prepared with tools to break down doors. However, one year some children got into the infants' classrooms through a toilet window and they made straight for those objects of fascination – the teachers' drawers. Mrs Snow and Miss Krantz both had their desks ransacked and the tins containing money were emptied. The intruders also threw sand all over the floor and scattered Miss Krantz's boxes of counters.

We usually have a pretty shrewd idea which boys have chosen to revisit us after dark, but none of them has ever been caught at it. And we know that once they become absorbed into the secondary school brotherhood they will move on to more demanding activities (like shop-breaking and motor cycle nobbling), and that we at St. Claude's will be left in peace until the following autumn, when the next lot will visit us.

But on one occasion we were broken into by people who came equipped not only with tools to break down doors, but also, apparently, sack-trucks to carry away the safe. These breakers made straight for the school office, the stock cupboard and Mr Masterton's room. They took away the photocopier, the projector, two radios and a record player as well as the safe. They opened up polythene containers of paint and glue which they poured all over the floor and Mr Masterton's desk; they found the large tubes of duplicating ink which they put on the floor, and then stamped upon. They turned over my stationery rack into the mess upon the floor, and walked over the scattered paper. They emptied the contents of my desk upon the floor and covered the pile with all the powdered paint they could find. They then tried (but failed) to set fire to the place. I gain a certain comfort from the fact that the photocopier was 'on the blink' and had been declared unrepairable; the projector and one of the radios was broken, and the record player (an old model) only worked on the 78 r.p.m. speed. Moreover the safe, when they eventually managed to blow it open, would have been found to contain £1.50 dinner money, £1.72$\frac{1}{2}$ p school fund, 60p staff tea fund, 1 broken digital watch (that had been found in the playground) and four spare violin strings (G).

Other visitors, who have no rights within the school but

who are not dishonest, are a bit of a nuisance sometimes because they take up time which I can't really afford them but which I feel, out of charity, obliged to give. There is a simple-minded lad of about 18 years who keeps on coming in to ask if we have a vacancy for a cleaner. I don't think he has had a job since he left school (and I wouldn't think he stands much chance of getting one) but he persistently visits all establishments within walking distance of his home, seeking work as a cleaner. Mr Potts always gravely interviews him, and promises to let him know if a suitable vacancy occurs . . . and I believe he would too. Then there are the people who try to sell us things, (one woman wanted to set up a stall in the playground, selling home-made flapjacks to the children; another woman visits us just before Christmas trying to sell dolls) and there is a little old lady from the nearby almshouses who just comes in because she is lonely and wants to chat. But bigger nuisances are the drunks who find their way into the school by mistake, and estranged parents who, separated from their families by a Court Order, try to pull a fast one by gaining access to their children at school.

Trying not to become involved in custody cases involves all Mr Masterton's tact and my skill in carefully wording his letters of reply to solicitors. If a custody case is being fought out Mr Masterton will always get letters from the solicitors representing each party – the one requesting confirmation that 'John is doing well at school and appears happy', and the other asking if 'John's unhappy home life is in any way reflected in his attainments at school'. Each solicitor will receive an identical letter which tries to tell the truth, without saying anything positive. But although the school wishes to remain aloof in the argument of who has the custody of John, we sometimes have to take positive action to prevent a breach of the law taking place. On one occasion I had an urgent call from a probation officer who telephoned from the Court to say that Mrs Perkins had just been awarded the custody of John, but that Mr Perkins had left the Court in a rage and it was suspected that he was on way to school to seize John, and would we please not let the child go. We hustled John Perkins out of Mrs Snow's class and into Mrs Potts' kitchen about two minutes before the fat, sweating and rather aggressive Mr Perkins marched into the office and demanded to know where John was. I told him that 'someone representing Mrs Perkins had already collected the child' . . . and sat at my desk hoping that Mr Perkins wasn't going to hit me.

In the absence of Mr Masterton it is me who copes with all these unwelcome day-time visitors, but undoubtedly it is the goings-on after dark that pose a bigger threat to the school, and as the security of the premises is Mr Potts' main responsibility he is naturally worried about the break-ins we occasionally suffer. We have no burglar alarm. (I don't think The Authority would even consider the expense of fitting burglar alarms to schools) but this fact doesn't concern Mr Potts as he guesses that, if installed, the thing would be sounding off every time a mouse nibbled a wire, but would remain silent when a window was broken. Mr Potts accepts that anyone determined to break into St. Claude's will find a way in somehow, and all he can do is to make the premises as secure as he can each night and hope for the best.

Mr Potts also worries about the gas central heating system. He wasn't happy when they installed it seven years ago (he much preferred the old coal-fired boiler that had been keeping St. Claude's warm since the 1920s) and he is always fearful that one day it will explode. As the new gas boiler is pumping very hot water around the original system of old pipes we get a lot of trouble with our central heating. We get frequent leaks, blockages and air-locks; the automatic timer tends to switch itself off when it shouldn't and fails to switch on when it should but, as yet, the thing hasn't exploded. I don't think that Mr Potts fully understands it. He knew where he was with a shovel, a furnace and a stack of coke; but fiddling with buttons and watching dials are alien tasks to him. He gets worried when lights show red when they shouldn't; he doesn't like to think of the thing operating under its own control at night; he is convinced the whole lot will go up in flames. And Mr Potts has no more faith in fire alarms than he has in burglar alarms.

The fire alarm system at St. Claude's used to be the simple clanging of a brass handbell. A few years ago The Authority decided that this was not adequate. (They're probably right; we use the same handbell to signify playtimes and the start and finish of the day's schooling.) So they installed an electric system which was operated by a button in the office. This alarm made an appalling Whee-Whaah-Wheeh-Whaah noise and worked perfectly efficiently on the occasions we used it for Fire Practice. But we only had it for 18 months. The Authority once more decided that the system was inadequate and that we should have one that would work from a standby battery as well as mains electricity, and so the new Whee-Whaah was ripped out and a newer one installed. This one has a large control panel in the office (with a multitude of buttons and lights) and alarm-raising buttons behind cover-glasses fixed to the walls in corridors throughout the school. It all looks very new, shiny and impressive – but it doesn't work, which is probably just as well because the children are always breaking the cover-glasses in the corridors. Visiting mechanics occasionally get a few Whee-Whaahs out of the thing, and go away assuring us that it's O.K. now, but each time we have tried it for a Fire Practice it hasn't worked. (When the last visiting mechanic was about to leave I pointed out to him that the 'Power-Supply-Healthy' green light still wasn't working. 'Oh that doesn't matter,' he said, 'it's only the bulb gone – and I haven't got a spare one on me.')

Fire practices are held once a term. The approach of a Governors' Meeting will usually remind Mr Masterton that a Fire Practice is due (a statement that the school was evacuated efficiently at the last Fire Practice is a routine part of his report) and he always arranges the practice to take place just before playtime so that the children, having been ushered out to the playgrounds, can stay there. Some Headteachers are not so considerate about Fire Practices. Some of them surprise their staff by never announcing in advance the date and time of a proposed practice, and I knew of one Head who was unsporting enough to occasionally seize and hide a child inside the school during the evacuation procedure in order to test whether the class teacher had, according to the rules, taken out the Class Register and checked off each child against it once the safety of the playground had been reached. Curiously, we have never felt obliged to try and sound the alarm for a real

147

fire – although it has been necessary to send for the Fire Brigade a couple of times.

Bearing in mind the dodgy state of the school's electrical wiring in general, the battered condition of all plugs and sockets, and the enthusiastic (but only nominally supervised) chemistry and cookery classes, it is surprising that we don't get frequent fires. We once had a scare when someone threw a firework into the stationery cupboard; and Mrs Beagle once got into a panic when there was a gas blow-back on her new chipper – but the only occasion recently when a fire was in danger of getting out of hand was during one of Mr Appleby's cookery classes which was being held in the staffroom. A crowd of children were standing around a pan of boiling toffee on the stove; someone was larking about with the gas lighter 'gun' – and the next moment the staffroom curtains were on fire. The mother who had been left in charge of the children could not think what to do so she rushed off to tell Mr Appleby. Mr Appleby pounded down the corridor to the staffroom, yelling at me, as he passed the office, to summon the Fire Brigade. I did so.

Now, alongside the stove, hanging on the wall, is an asbestos blanket secured in a heavy-duty plastic bag. Hanging from the bottom of the bag are two red tapes and the idea is that in an emergency you yank on the tapes and release the blanket. Mr Appleby yanked. The entire blanket pack came off the wall, complete with Rawlplugs and a shower of plaster, but the blanket stayed firmly inside its tough polythene sheath. No amount of clawing at it managed to release the blanket, so Mr Appleby threw it aside and got to work with wet tea towels. By the time the Fire Brigade arrived Mr Appleby had in fact managed to tear down the staffroom curtains which were now a smouldering mess on the floor. It was then that we remembered the pan of toffee, which was now smoking blackly on the stove. The firemen stayed to have coffee – the children were allowed to crawl all over the fire engine and play with the siren and the public address system (much to the annoyance of at least one local resident who came to the office to complain, as her husband was on night duty and trying to sleep) and, on the whole, the episode ended quite happily for everyone except for Mr and Mrs

Potts who had to clear up the mess in the staffroom.

I once had to send for the Police Bomb Squad. It happened upon one gentle summer's afternoon when I was absorbed in the task of removing caked mud and withered corpses from the Wormery, and Mr Masterton was sitting quietly in his office working on a new timetable. The telephone rang. I answered it and a child's voice said, 'There's a bomb in your school.' I said 'Hello? Who's that? Who's that speaking' – but the receiver the other end was replaced. I sat there thinking awhile and decided that it was a childish hoax that should be ignored. But then I had doubts. Suppose . . . suppose it was *genuine*? I went in to see Mr Masterton. 'Well, it's obviously some child playing a trick,' he said, 'it would be ridiculous to take any action on a thing like that.' Then he thoughtfully rubbed his chin. 'On the other hand,' he pondered, 'I suppose I shouldn't ignore it. I mean to say; just suppose it were *genuine*. I think, on reflection, you had better seek advice from the police station.'

I decided not to treat this as an emergency, so I didn't dial 999 but I rang the local police station. The officer in charge snorted. 'I don't really think you need worry,' he said. 'It's obviously some little layabout sitting bored at home who thinks he'll get you going.' 'So you think we should ignore it,' I said. There was an awkward pause. Then a sigh. 'I suppose we *ought* to treat it seriously,' said the officer. 'After all, we'd all look rather foolish if it *was* genuine.'

I went around the classes in turn and muttered an explanation to each teacher. Some of Mr Appleby's class were having a cookery lesson in the staffroom. 'But what about our sponge cakes?' wailed the mum in charge, 'they've only just gone into the oven!' She looked at her watch. 'How long are we going to have to stand outside?' 'Until the bomb goes off,' I said, turning off the oven. Within ten minutes all the children were assembled against the far wall of the playground, and the police were inside the building making a search. Mr Potts, who was off duty at the time and had to be fetched from home, handed over all his keys and then came and joined us in the playground. We pretended to the children that it was another version of Fire Practice, but somehow they got to know what it was all about. 'There's a bomb! . . . Where's the bomb? . . . We've got a bomb!' They were all hopping about with excitement. After twenty minutes the police came out and said that the school was safe, and we all trooped back inside. The cookery mum, who looked on the point of tears, glanced at me reproachfully and rushed back into the staffroom.

Just before going-home time the same afternoon the telephone rang again. 'There's a bomb in your school,' said a childish voice . . .

CHAPTER TEN

Money Matters

One day an old man came into the office dragging behind him a shopping basket on wheels. The shopping basket was obviously heavy and the old man had obviously struggled up the hill with it. I sat him down and waited whilst he mopped his brow and gathered his breath. The shopping basket was full of red books. When he had recovered sufficiently to be able to talk, the old man explained that he was moving from his flat to an old people's home and so had to get rid of most of his possessions . . . 'and I know schools are short of money and can't afford to buy books, so I thought you might like these.' 'These' was a complete set of books by Charles Dickens. The set was a Book Club edition, printed in the 1930s – and their red covers a little faded now, but the titles were embossed clearly in gold, and the books were lavishly illustrated with prints of the original drawings by Phiz. The old man took them from his basket and placed them carefully upon my desk. One or two of them had covers that were stained slightly by damp, and one cover was broken. 'They've had a bit of use mind,' he said, 'and I shall miss not having them around; but then – the print's too small for me these days anyway.' He paused, with his hand still on the pile of books, 'and I'm glad to be able to present them to the school.'

I made the old man a cup of tea, and then introduced him to Mr Masterton, who shook him warmly by the hand and expressed the school's gratitude for such a generous gift. The old man went happily on his way, trailing his empty basket, and Mr Masterton came out into my office and stared at the pile of books on my desk. He picked up *Oliver Twist*, and then flipped casually through *The Pickwick Papers*. 'Put them in the stock cupboard for now,' he said. 'We might get a few pence for them at the next Jumble Sale.'

In these days of national stringency and local government financial difficulty it is a commonly held belief that all schools are short of money. The cash allocation to each school is normally based upon the number of children on roll and at St. Claude's we manage very well thank you on ours. In fact (between you and me) we have too much money and as the end of each financial year approaches Mr Masterton has to urge the staff to look around their classrooms to see what they need in order that we spend out (or, preferably, overspend) our allocation. He knows perfectly well that any money left against St. Claude's balance at the end of the year will not be allowed to accumulate and will be taken off our allocation for the next year – and he is fearful that The Authority may get the idea we don't need all this money and reduce our allocation accordingly.

When I read in the newspapers of other schools in such desperate financial straits that children are having to share half a pencil each and write on toilet paper I am completely baffled. Where on earth do they go wrong? It isn't as though we, at St. Claude's, are particularly watchful of expense. Certainly Miss Krantz and Mr Singleton are inclined to be rather parsimonious when ordering equipment, but their frugal attitudes are more than off-set by the carefree extravagance of the others. And it's obvious from the stack of abandoned and unwanted equipment in the stock cupboard that this free and easy spending has been going on at St. Claude's for many years. During the past couple of decades there have been quite a few changes of staff at St. Claude's and each new teacher has brought with him or her an enthusiasm for a certain subject or teaching method.

We have, for example, had bright young teachers who were 'into' craft work, modelling, multi-link mathematics and nature study. The teachers have long since left us but their stacks of Swedish looms, broken spinning wheels, boxes of balsa wood, sanding sticks, multi-link cubes, microscopes and vasculums are still with us. The layers recede dimly to the back of the cupboard. Just inside the door you will catch your legs in the plastic-coated wires of the storage display frames and 6' high wire book-rack ordered last year by a teacher who liked all books and equipment on show . . . and lost in the dust somewhere at the back of the cupboard is the teaching machine and stack of programmed textbooks that date from St. Claude's first steps into 'progressive' education during the 1960s. In order to get to the safe I have to ease past a 4' x 4' pegboard exhibition screen, and yesterday I put my foot in a fish tank that someone had dumped on the floor. When Mr Scott leaves (he's been with us for two years now, and so has started to look at the Vacancy Bulletin each week) I will give the cupboard contents a gentle but firm shove and, somewhere on a shelf or in a box, find room for all the electronic gadgetry in his classroom. No-one else in the school wants it, and Mr Scott's successor will have entirely new ideas. (In my experience each new teacher has discarded the equipment – and criticised the teaching methods – of the preceding teacher.)

In order to keep the school interested in spending money, the purveyors of school equipment bombard us each year with catalogues. The catalogues are large, heavy and printed on glossy paper. The photographs are first-class, the drawings accurate, the text instructive and the indexes comprehensive. They are, in themselves, articles of very high quality. The goods they are hoping to persuade us to buy are not. Mostly made of crudely moulded plastics, or constructed of flimsy and splintery plywoods, these artifacts of learning are more often than not shoddy bits of rubbish that fall to pieces or crack up soon after the children get their hands upon them. But Mrs Snow, Mr Scott and Mr Appleby are not dismayed. They love browsing through the catalogues, so when items of their equipment fall to pieces they simply leaf through the latest brochure and then send for something else.

When the goods arrive at the office I unpack them with cynicism. I know what they cost – and I am always appalled. But they are always beautifully packaged. Surrounded with a sea of plastic foam chips, sheathed in polythene wraps, held in moulded polystyrene shapes, protected by corrugated heavy-duty paper and finally secured in stout cardboard boxes bound with inviolable plastic strips, this pseudo-educational trash comes to us cherished by expensive, imaginative packaging that ensures its safe transportation. Recently Mrs Snow sent for a replacement Tiny Tots Trundle Trolley. It came in the form of a kit which consisted of several pieces of plywood (splintering at the edges and broken at one corner), several pieces of dowel (which were meant to slot into holes which didn't line up) a sealed polythene packet of screws and four Shepherd's castors. I suggested to Mrs Snow that she abandoned the plywood and dowel and fastened the Shepherd's castors onto the cardboard box the outfit came in, which would provide an excellent Trundle Trolley for Tiny Tots. She thought I was joking.

I find that teachers' attitudes to educational equipment varies – usually in accordance with their age. Those under 40, who have grown up in a consumer society that accepts manufactured trumpery as normal, are usually light-hearted about things that don't work or don't last and have to be thrown away within a few months of purchase. Those over 40, who have known a world that expects better standards, grumble and sometimes go to great lengths to avoid buying something new. The episode of Mr Singleton and the pin-hole camera is a good example of these two attitudes.

Mr Singleton runs a lunchtime club for juniors. The activity of the club varies from year to year – according to the talents and interests of the juniors who want to join. (Last year, for example, it was chess; this year – and probably next too – the enthusiastic recorder players take up Mr Singleton's club time.) A few years ago the club activity was photography and, under Mr Singleton's guidance, all of the twelve juniors taking part made themselves a pin-hole camera. First of all they were told to bring in a tin of suitable shape which had a fitting lid. Those children who were unable to find a cocoa tin or toffee tin that would serve the purpose were each provided with an old tin tea caddy from a stock which Mr Singleton had obviously been hoarding at home.

Over the next few weeks the lunchtime photography club received instruction on basic photography in Mr

Singleton's classroom; they made their cameras in the Art Room; they photographed each other in the playground, and they processed their negatives in the Medical Room – which served as the dark room when the window was blacked out with the army blankets. Each child made its camera by punching a hole in the end of the tin with a nail; covering the hole with a piece of kitchen foil secured inside the tin with Sellotape; painting the inside of the tin with old blackboard paint (found by Mr Singleton at the back of the stock cupboard); piercing the foil carefully with a fine needle and finally constructing a 'shutter' by simply covering the outside of the punched hole with a strip of plastic electrical insulating tape. In the Medical Room (which was temporarily lit with a red bulb from an abandoned electric fire) the children cut pieces of photographic bromide paper to fit their cameras, and then marched out to the playground to take it in turns to photograph each other by lifting their insulating-tape shutters and exposing their 'film' for a length of time prescribed by Mr Singleton. Each child processed its own negative in the Medical Room – and returned the following week to print the photograph.

During the course of that year those pin-hole cameras were used a lot. Some children were interested enough to experiment with them at home, and they brought in their photographs for Mr Singleton's praise and criticism. The cost of this club to the school was less than £1. The photographic paper was a packet of out of date single-weight paper bought cheaply at a local shop, the developing dishes were enamelled pie dishes borrowed from Mrs Beagle, the children used plastic clothes pegs as tongs to lift their bits of paper from the dishes, and the photographic chemicals themselves were given by Mr Singleton . . . and a long time he must have had them too, because I noticed that the Fixer was in a jar labelled 'Hypo – 1/6d'.

Now this term we have a young student with us for teaching practice. It is customary for such student teachers to be attached to a certain class and to lead a 'project' for the children within that class. Our student, Josephine, is attached to Mr Appleby's class. Her particular interest is, she says, physics and she first of all chose as her project pin-hole photography. Mr Singleton (prepared to be interested and encouraging) brought to school one of the pin-hole cameras that a child had made for his lunchtime club. But Josephine didn't want to know anything about Mr Singleton's pin-hole camera. She handled it briefly, suppressed a giggle, and then gave it back to him saying that it wasn't really necessary for her to go to all that trouble because *'you can get a pack these days'*. Mr Singleton said nothing. He took the camera home again and has never mentioned the subject again.

Josephine sent for her 'pack' and it arrived a week later. It consisted of lots of pieces of black paper to be stuck together to form cameras, together with a sheet of instructions. Josephine was prepared to use the army-blanket-darkened Medical Room, but she didn't want Mr Singleton's old electric fire bulb (which was back in the stock cupboard). 'I want to do the job *properly*,' she explained. So Josephine bought a 'safe lamp', four plastic developing dishes, a thermometer, some print tongs, packets of developer and fixer chemicals, and a 100-sheet pack of the latest 'resin-coated' photographic paper. The children working on Josephine's project assembled their paper cameras under her instructions, but unfortunately they were so flimsy that when being handled in the playground the paper seams gaped and let in the light, so the first set of negatives had to be scrapped. Josephine spent the next few dinner hours in the staffroom strengthening the cameras with bits of cardboard and gluing all the seams together in order to exclude all light.

I understand that some photographs were eventually taken, but none of us ever saw the results and as the light-secure cameras had to be torn to bits in order to get out the exposed negatives, they were only used the once and ended up as so much torn paper in my wastebin. I don't know whether any of Mr Appleby's children have learned anything about photography (Josephine's project has now moved on to other areas of 'light' understanding – last week she sent for a set of Perspex colour prisms) but her experiment cost the school. £29.32, and the safe lamp, developing dishes, thermometer and print tongs are now in a box (behind the fish tank) in the stock cupboard.

The glossy catalogue advertisers are not allowed to lure

the school into buying *all* equipment and materials from them. Certain basics – like paper, exercise books, pencils, pens, kitchen and school cleaning equipment – have to be purchased, by arrangement of The Authority, from a large consortium which supplies all these things to most schools in this part of Britain. We are supplied with a double-foolscap size, 12-page, closely printed order form which we have to complete and send off once a term. Each member of staff has to anticipate his or her needs for the next term, and hand me a list of the things wanted. My job is to correlate all these requests onto the one order form. And when the goods ordered from the consortium eventually arrive at the school Mr Masterton and I have the mammoth task of dishing it all out.

Sometimes little mistakes are made. Like the time Mr Singleton received five dozen letter openers instead of the five dozen H.B. pencils he had ordered (because I had mis-read one of those closely printed lines on the order form) and the time Mrs Beagle wanted to know what the hell she was supposed to do with twelve polythene cartons of playing-field-marking-out paint (which had been delivered to the wrong school). In order to offer for sale these cheaper than average goods the consortium has to scour world markets for their supplies and this, in itself, can lead to problems.

Sometimes very big mistakes are made. Like the time all schools received an urgent message to withdraw from circulation certain pencils of a particular colour of Far-Eastern origin (because they were apparently covered with lead paint and alleged to be injurious to anyone who chewed them); and the time we had a similar panic-laden instruction to destroy certain First Aid 'sterile' dressings of Middle-Eastern origin (because they had been found to be contaminated by typhoid, Bubonic plague and God-knows-what-else). However, most of the consortium's ill-judged purchases are inconvenient rather than dangerous – like the batch of extra-cheap pencils that snapped under the slightest pressure, and the consignment of anti-dust chalk, the description of which was so impressive that we sent for two hundred boxes. The chalk was certainly anti-dust; but it was also anti-blackboard. No-one has yet been able to get anything more than a few greasy smears from this chalk and so all two hundred boxes are now abandoned on a shelf in the stock cupboard.

But on the whole, mistakes notwithstanding, the consortium system seems to be a more efficient way of supplying schools than leaving every purchasing decision to the teaching staff who, in my experience, are not very wise shoppers. Mr Masterton, for example, has a *thing* about discount. He will allow no-one to buy anything from anywhere unless he can be guaranteed a 'school's discount', even though it sometimes means travelling further and paying much more for goods that could have been bought from the shop around the corner that doesn't give discount.

The money which The Authority allocates us has to be spent upon equipment and materials which are considered essential, or desirable, for the purpose of educating the children. Money needed for things like outings, Christmas presents for the infants, prizes for Sports Day, and food for the gerbil, rabbit and budgerigar has to come from the School Fund – and raising money for the School Fund takes up a lot of everyone's time.

Many schools expect parents to contribute a small, regular amount each term towards the School Fund, but at St. Claude's the pressure upon parents to do so is very light indeed. Each teacher (with the exception of Mr Singleton) keeps a tin labelled 'School Fund' which is sometimes rattled in front of parents who come in to the classroom, but we are lucky if we raise as much as £5.00 a term in this way. (Mr Singleton objects to parents being asked to contribute to School Fund and refuses to keep such a tin upon his desk.) The least troublesome way of raising money is to charge 10p or 15p admission to parents who attend our termly concerts or plays. But as the mothers most likely to attend such events are those who are already involved in the production as 'helpers' and don't therefore feel they should have to pay an admission fee On the Night, our takings at these performances are sometimes a little meagre. Undoubtedly our main money-raising events of the year are the Summer 'Fayre' and Christmas Bazaar (spelled 'bazzar' if Mr Scott makes the posters).

Our Summer Fayre is held at the school every year on the Saturday nearest to 21st June. Preparations for it start immediately after Easter. First of all a staff meeting is held to decide who is doing what on the day – for example, last year Mrs Snow ran the the the toddlers' 'As-Nu' stall, Miss Krantz the cake stall, Mr Scott the White Elephant stall, Mr Singleton the Book stall (Mr Singleton *always* runs the Book stall), Mr Appleby looked after the Fun-and-Games stand – and then I send out letters to parents asking for *their* co-operation. Every year we need volunteers for the Bottle stall, the Guess-the-cake-weight stand, the Tombola, the Lucky Dip and a brave person to assist Mr Appleby on the Fun-and-Games stand. (As most of the test-your-strength or try-your-skill equipment on the Fun-and-Games stand was made by Mr Appleby and has been known to give out splinters, cuts and electric shocks it *needs* to be a brave person who assists him.) At one time we also had a candy-floss machine and a pop-corn making machine (both made by Mr Appleby), but as one year the candy-floss machine flew in bits and sprayed the corridor and a queue of children with sticky pink fluff, and on another occasion the pop-corn machine caught fire, they both have now been abandoned. (About two-thirds the way back in the stock cupboard I think.)

As the Fayre date draws nearer I will send out requests for contributions to the 'As-Nu', White Elephant and Book stalls and I clear a space in the office to receive it all. Those who bring worthwhile and useful articles will come across to my desk and draw my attention to the gift they are offering; those who are using the Fayre as a dumping ground for accumulated rubbish will sneak in with large bulging plastic carrier bags which they slide into a corner before making off. We know in advance the sort of things that will come; and we also know the sort of people who will bring them.

Parents Type 1 will bring a small quantity of very high quality wool, silk, linen or cotton clothing (obviously second-hand but cared-for, sometimes with a neat darn or patch – beautifully laundered), a spin dryer, electric fire or toaster (probably dating from the 1950s or 60s, but in perfect working order), and a selection of clean and cared-for books. Parents Type 2 will bring large bags of equally good quality clothing (but crumpled, sometimes dirty, and with a few buttons missing) and piles of magazines. They will bring lampshades, shoes, hand-woven baskets, pieces of odd-shaped home-made pottery, and many boxes of children's games — parts of which will be missing. Any item of electrical equipment from this group will be last year's model — broken. Parents Type 4 will bring china ornaments, knitted teacosies and toilet roll covers, and children's clothing – mostly made of nylon, almost new and carefully wrapped in tissue paper. Parents Type 3 and 5 bring nothing.

When the sea of collected boxes, books and bags in my office gets to the unmanageable stage I start nagging the others to come and collect the items appropriate to their stall and transfer them to their classrooms. And for a week prior to Fayre Day each classroom resembles a junk shop as the goods are sorted, assembled and priced between (and during) lessons. My last job is to duplicate hundreds of little notes advertising the event. Each child will leave clutching a dozen or so notes some of which will, hopefully, be pushed through the letter boxes of the houses on the way home from school.

On the Saturday itself Mr Potts will open up the school at about 10.30 a.m. The Fayre won't start until after lunch, but we need the morning to clear the classrooms and set up the stalls. Parents will start drifting in early, to set up their stands and bring last-minute cakes from their freezers for Miss Krantz's stall. Mrs Beagle will be in her kitchen early to make the batches of buns, doughnuts and scones, which she sells (with Mrs Pin's assistance) at a fantastic rate and with a fantastic profit, along with cups of tea or coffee. The School Fund always buys the tea, coffee and sugar for Mrs Beagle's Summer Fayre refreshments, but she has never requested ingredients for her cakes. We don't know how she manages to fiddle them – and we don't ask. My particular job on the day is to sell raffle tickets and give out change. Mr Masterton breezes around 'being available'.

By about 5.30 p.m. the last customer has trailed away; we are all exhausted; the school is in a mess . . . and we have probably made about £300. The takings of the White Elephant stall and Mrs Beagle's refreshments are good, and the cake stall always sells out. Everyone is usually pleased with the amount of money they have taken, with the exception of Mr Singleton who seems to end up with almost as many books upon his stall as he started with. All the left-over books, clothes and white elephants are bundled together and shoved into the Jumble Cupboard to await the next fund-raising occasion. (The Christmas Bazaar – with the addition of Father Christmas in his Gift Grotto – follows exactly the same pattern as the Summer Fayre.)

Jumble Sales are arranged once a term and they are organised entirely by helpful mums. They are held in the Assembly Hall upon a chosen week-day, immediately after school. My only concern with these affairs is that, once again, the office is the collecting point for the clothes, shoes, old lawn mowers, hair dryers, toys, magazines, push-chairs and rusting oil stoves, etc. The only difference between this lot and the last lot is that the jumble is always scruffier and smellier. Quite often items brought at one jumble sale will reappear for the sale again at the next. There is a pair of outsize men's black serge trousers and a broken vacuum cleaner that have turned up at each jumble sale held at the school for the last four years.

Another way in which schools can raise money is by acting as agents for firms who wish to sell things to the parents of schoolchildren; things like fluorescent safety-first duffle bags or armbands; name-tapes; photographs. The idea is that the school gets a discount on all items sold, and a very good idea this is for all concerned, except me. I have to do all the work. I don't so much mind selling the fluorescent bags – where at least the parents, having been shown a sample, have to pay in advance and no nonsense. But sorting out the arguments over name-tapes, and chasing up the photograph-payment defaulters are time-consuming activities that I can well do without. The trouble with the name-tapes is that they take about two months to arrive, by which time some parents have mis-remembered what they ordered. ('Surely I said I wanted *Samuel J.* Broadworthy, and not just *Sam* Broadworthy?') Also, the names come on one long roll of tape and I have to spend a whole afternoon cutting them up and putting them into separate plastic envelopes with a sheet of instructions . . . and sometimes the firm makes a mistake with spelling and tapes have to be sent back. But at least, like the duffle bags, name-tapes have to be paid for in advance so I have no accounting to do – which is the major problem with the photographs.

The school photographer comes once a year and takes a picture of each beaming class, with the teacher standing alongside. The children love the occasion because the taking of the photograph provides a welcome diversion; the teachers love it because they get a free photo; Mr Masterton loves it because we get a handsome 20% on all photographs sold. I don't love it at all. I know that about three weeks after the photographer's visit a large parcel of photographs will arrive: one for each child in the school, and one for each member of staff. None of these photographs has been paid for in advance, and I am given an invoice, a pre-paid reply label, and a sheet of instructions. Each child is given its photograph to take home to show Mum. If Mum likes it she is supposed to send back the money for it; if Mum doesn't like it she is supposed to send back the photograph. Nowhere in the instructions does it tell me what I am supposed to do about the mum who keeps the photo but doesn't send in the money, or about the child who loses the photo on the way home.

In my opinion the amount of money we make over these sales-in-school ventures does not justify the amount of time spent on them (and I'm not sure that it's entirely ethical anyway; it amounts to The Authority, in paying my wages to do other people's clerical work and debt-collecting, subsidising the firms involved) and I have told Mr Masterton that I could make more money for the school, with less strain on my nerves, if only he would hire me out once or twice a term to the local secretarial agency.

So, with a generous financial allocation from The Authority each year (always referred to, in educational jargon, as 'capitation') and a healthy balance in our School Fund, we at St. Claude's lack for nothing that money can buy. But you could be forgiven for thinking that we were, in fact, crippled with poverty if you visited the school and saw the crumbling state of our roofs and stonework, our rotting woodwork and our peeling paintwork. This is because payment for maintenance of school buildings comes from The Authority's central education funds, not from 'capitation' and The Authority's education funds are, we are told, at an all-time low. Because of this shortage of money The Authority is constantly thinking up ways of saving it – not only by annually reviewing each school's capitation allowance (against which, of course, all Headteachers take appropriate defensive action) but also by introducing money-saving schemes. Like the taps, for instance.

One afternoon last year a little man carrying a clipboard and toolbag came into the office and said he had come to change the taps. I was puzzled. I told him that we had multiple roof leaks, a swimming pool out of action because of electrical and ceiling problems, a dangerously cracked wall, and a blocked drain in the playground but we did *not* have, so far as I was aware, any trouble with the taps. The little man didn't know anything about roof leaks or cracked walls. All he knew was that we had to have all our taps changed for reasons of 'water economy'. Our school still had the old high-pressure screw-down bib-cock taps (the ones you have to turn) which had all to be changed to the non-concussive spring press-down self-closing type (the ones you have to lean on). He had a sheaf of documents on his clipboard listing the schools that had to be done and, sure enough, St. Claude's was amongst them. He was with us for four and a half days and at lunchtime on the Friday it took the children about 10 seconds to discover a new game. You stand to one side of the sink and, calling out to an unsuspecting child to 'come and see the new taps' you wait until the child is standing against the sink and then you press down the tap. The water, coming out in a high-speed gush, strikes the curved surface of the wash hand basin, then swooshes up the side and drenches the front of the child standing there.

For several weeks after the fitting of the new taps the corridor wash hand basins were a major focal point during playtimes and dinnertimes. The corridor floor was awash all the way up to the classrooms, and practically all the children sat down to the afternoon session with soaking wet tummies. If these sinks were fitted with plugs (they are not because as fast as Mr Potts replaces them they disappear again) and if such plugs were used (I am sure that they would not be) then I can see that there would be some saving of water. But, as things are, they are splashy nuisances that have only one advantage; at least the children can't leave them running.

The splashy nuisance fitted in the staff cloakroom had no advantages whatsoever and I, particularly, found it trying. On the day it was installed, for example, I had occasion to do a particularly mucky job sorting out a crumpled stencil on the duplicator. I elbowed my way into the cloakroom with filthy ink-stained hands and with the heel of my left hand I applied pressure to the hot tap. I received a scalding jet of water into my right hand which catapulted the soap from my grasp and soaked the front of my skirt. I didn't get on much better with the cold tap and eventually said to hell with this and, without a twinge of conscience, groped for the machine-dispensed roller towel (which had run out long since anyway) and to the filthy dangling end (which bore the clay-daubed handmarks of Mr Appleby) I added my splurge of black inky fingermarks. We asked Mr Potts if he could find us a plug for the sink, but he went one better. He found us an old brass screw-down bib-cock tap with which he replaced the new tap . . . and we are now back to normal in the staff toilet.

Another economy measure was the 'SAVE IT' electricity campaign. The Authority sent us some posters for our notice board, a lot of little sticky labels saying 'SWITCH IT OFF' for us to stick beside all light-switches, and an 'I'M AN ENERGY SAVER' badge for each child in the school. The children loved their badges, but they soon lost them and we were unable to obtain replacements. The 'SAVE IT' electricity campaign only lasted one term. I suppose The Authority found it too expensive.

The Authority's latest idea for saving money is to extend the Christmas holiday period by one week and to deduct one week from the summer holiday so that staff and pupils are keeping warm at home for an extra week during the winter, thus saving The Authority a week of heating costs. They tried it for the first time last winter. Last winter was severe – and The Authority found that those schools whose caretakers economised during the holiday by turning off their heating incurred expensive repair bills because of burst pipes; and those schools that didn't suffer burst pipes were those whose caretakers (Mr Potts amongst them) wasted The Authority's money by maintaining warm but empty schools.

However, economy meaures notwithstanding, The Authority remains short of money to spend on things like the maintenance of school buildings. It is little wonder that people who notice the dilapidated state of the local school are concerned that society may be scrimshanking over the education of children.

But . . . coming back to that old man with his basket of red books, you will be pleased to know that his gift was not in fact wasted. Mr Singleton (who appreciates a good Phiz when he sees one) seized the lot when they were offered to him for his Summer Fayre Book Stall, and he contributed £1 towards the School Fund. When Mr Singleton retires next year I know that the complete set of Dickens will go with him; but in the meantime they are on the shelf behind his desk and I have no doubt at all that his class will be introduced to them. And that would certainly please the old man.

CHAPTER ELEVEN

Festivals

It seems to me that the rhythm of the educational year within our state primary schools has remained unchanged since the Education Act of 1870. Today's values and attitudes, of society in general and teachers in particular, would no doubt be incomprehensible to a headmaster of the early 1900s, but he would be reassured to know that the Harvest Thanksgiving of Autumn will be followed by the festivites at Christmas; that the Resurrection and Ascension will be observed (after a fashion) at Eastertime, and that the treats and sports day in July will be followed by the long summer holiday. The children still follow their ritual observance of skipping and hop-scotch seasons, and some of the clapping and chanting games of the playground are as permanent as time itself. The teaching staff still make benevolent allowance for conker time, bonfire night and Hallowe'en, and the encouragement of 'nature study' runs as a continuous theme throughout the school year.

But during the first three weeks of September there is more straightforward, uninterrupted, honest-to-goodness basic educational hard work carried out in the classrooms at St. Claude's than in any other period of the academic year. The teaching staff – refreshed and restored after their holidays – are enthusiastic to start new projects; the children – most of whom have become so bored with the holidays that coming to school is almost a novelty – are in the right frame of mind to concentrate; and the school – having received its annual clean and polish – is sweet-

166

smelling and welcoming. The first non-academic occasion (Harvest Festival) is still many weeks away and, most important of all, there are no *visitors*.

Towards the end of September the official visitors will start arriving. Bringing with them their film strips and posters, they will come from the Royal Society for the Prevention of Accidents, the Drug Abuse Monitoring Unit,* the Dental Hospital, British Rail, the Fire Brigade, the Police Station and other worthy organisations for the purpose of persuading the children to mind the traffic, avoid sniffing glue, clean their teeth, keep off railway lines, not to play with matches and not to go with strangers, etc. Towards the end of September, also, will come the students – those who wish to have teaching practice – those who wish to 'observe' – and those who wish to borrow a group of children to work with/psychologically test/ photograph/talk to, because of a thesis they are doing. But during the first three weeks of September the universities and polytechnics are still on holiday, and the official visitors from Worthy Organisations haven't woken up yet to the fact that *we* are back. So the lessons at St. Claude's continue uninterrupted.

The first festival of the school year is Harvest Thanksgiving, and at the end of September a staff meeting will be called by Mr Masterton to discuss the arrangements. We always (of course) have a food theme at our Harvest Festivals. For example, one year it was Dairy Products and a very nice lady from the Milk Marketing Board came along to talk to the children, and another year it was Sugar all Over the World and someone from the Sugar Corporation agreed to visit. Sometimes we make mistakes (like the year it was Farm Produce, and a man from a large bacon consortium gave us a completely unintelligible lecture on international marketing procedures) and sometimes we get bonuses (like the year it was Our Daily Bread and a nice lady from Hovis gave each child in the school a miniature loaf to take home). Every year at the staff meeting someone will suggest that it would

* A letter from the Drug Abuse Monitoring Unit is currently pinned to our notice board alongside an announcement from the Work Experience on Employers' Premises project. The juxtaposition of initials of these two government Bodies exhorts the reader to WEEP DAMU . . .

be nice to have some 'new' music for a change, and every year this suggestion is brushed aside by Mr Singleton who insists upon We Plough the Fields and Scatter, Come ye Thankful People Come and Summer Suns are Glowing.

Once the theme is decided upon and the date of the Harvest Festival fixed, each teacher must go away and think up a theme-related project that the class will work upon in the weeks ahead. The theme of Our Daily Bread, which comes around once every six years or so, is one which Mrs Potts dreads because there will always be at least one class teacher who thinks it a good idea for the class to make bread as part of the project, and it usually takes Mrs Potts the rest of the term to sort out the dough-encrusted dishcloths, tea towels, chair covers and floor matting in the staffroom.

During the week before the Festival I will send out notes to the parents asking them to send in their gifts, and I prepare a space in the office to receive them. They come with the same predictability as the gifts for the Summer Fayre and Jumble Sales. Parents Type 1 usually accompany their children to the office bringing large and decorative baskets of fruit, or beautifully arranged sheaves of flowers; Parents Type 2 send in marrows or a bunch of turnips from their allotment or rusty tins of Yugoslavian peaches or suspect jars of aging shell-fish from the backs of their kitchen cupboards. Parents Type 4 send large tins of mixed fruit salad, or baked beans, packets of biscuits and bumper packs of crisps. Parents Types 3 and 5 usually send nothing.

Mrs Richardson always sends in an expertly baked Dundee fruit cake, covered in almonds, and another parent (who is in the bakery business) always makes the Harvest Loaf. The Harvest Loaf, symbolising all that is wholesome and nutritious from the good earth, is baked in the shape of a wheatsheaf, 2′ high and 3″ thick, covered with a sort of brown glaze and strengthened with cardboard and glue at the back. (After an unfortunate incident one year when one of the juniors was sick after stealing a corner of it, I have since taken the precaution of sticking a notice on the back of the Harvest Loaf to the effect that under no circumstances can it be eaten.)

One year, because of some obscure link with bees-and-honey, a parent brought in a wasps' nest which she thought might make an interesting decoration to our Harvest Festival platform. She explained that it had been removed from their loft. The loft had been fumigated and the wasps were all dead, but she felt that the nest was too interesting an object to destroy. I agreed with her; it certainly was an extraordinary thing . . . a great mushroom-like dome measuring about 4' in diameter and 3' in height, in creamy fawn waves of feather-like construction. She had the nest balanced upon a large piece of cardboard, and when I took it from her I nearly fell over because the thing was so light. I placed it on the table beside my desk, and everyone who came into the office peered at it in fascination. It was later on, during Assembly, when the school was quiet and I was absorbed in the task of adding up a column of figures that I heard the first buzz. I stared at the thing at my elbow in alarm. Surely I was mistaken? I carried on working and then, about ten minutes later, I heard another buzz; a long-drawn-out angry buzz this time, accompanied by a slight rustling scratching sound.

I picked up the nest carefully on its cardboard tray and carried it into Mr Masterton's room. I placed it upon his side table and came out again and shut the door. When Mr Masterton came back from Assembly I explained to him that I thought the nest had better stay in his room because the children were unable to keep their fingers from it and the nest was so fragile it could easily become damaged. He agreed with me at the time, but when I came back from lunch that afternoon I found the nest back in my office again, and Mr Masterton explained that he felt, on reflection, that it was a shame to keep such an interesting object in his office where very few people would see it and that it should stay on general view in my office.

The situation came to a head the next morning when Mrs Beagle – walking past the nest on her way to my desk to collect the dinner numbers – suddenly gave a sideways leap and said, 'That bloody thing's buzzing!' Mr Potts, who happened to be in the office at the time, said, 'I was beginning to have doubts about it myself; I had to get four wasps out of here this morning.' Mr Masterton, who would have heard this conversation from his office, came out and joined us. 'I think that most of the children have now seen it,' he said to Mr Potts. 'Perhaps you would like to get rid of it.' Mr Potts looked him straight in the eye. 'How?' This had us all silently thinking for a minute and then I suggested that we offered it to the Natural History Department of the City Museum. Everyone thought this was a brilliant idea except the museum when I rang them. They already had a perfect specimen of a wasps' nest thank you very much and didn't want another. I then had my second brilliant idea of the day and suggested that as the children of St. Claude's had all now seen it, should we perhaps let Commercial Street School have it? Mr Masterton said 'Excellent thinking' and told me to put the wasps' nest in his car. He then had second thoughts and told me to put it into Mr Appleby's car. 'Ron can take it over at lunchtime,' he explained. 'The nest will go through his hatch-back quite easily, whereas it might get damaged in my boot.'

The Harvest Festival service is always held in the afternoon, and Miss Krantz will spend the whole lunch break decorating the stage in the Assembly Hall. She does this extremely well. Apples, oranges, and tinned food will be displayed tumbling in cornucopian style from propped-up wastepaper baskets. These will be flanked by the marrows, onions and bunches of carrots. At the far sides of the display flowers will be banked, and she always finds some ivy to trail along the front. The centrepiece is, of course, the gleaming, crusty and inedible Harvest Loaf, backed by branches of copper beech, horse chestnut and sprigs of rosemary.

Last year Mr Singleton introduced a charming variation to the service. Mrs Snow's class (each child dressed in its best clothes) was kept in an excited whispering huddle at the back of the hall, and then during the singing of 'Come ye Thankful People Come' the children walked in solemn single file down the centre gangway carrying packets of tea, small tins of food, or an orange. As they reached the display each child placed its offering upon the pile in front of the Harvest Loaf and then scurried away to where Mrs Snow was waiting for them at the side of the stage. I had nipped up from the office in order to see part of the service and I stood just inside the doors squashed in beside Mrs Potts, Mrs Pin and Mrs Beagle. Mrs Beagle, smelling

170

faintly of Chloros bleach, had her large pink arms folded across her bosom, but as the little ones passed us, each carefully holding its Harvest Gift, she groped for her handkerchief. The service ended with a rousing chorus of We Plough the Fields and Scatter, and those of us standing at the back made our escape before the parents started moving from their seats. Mrs Beagle blew her nose. 'Talking about scattering seed,' she mumbled gruffly, 'those bloody mice have been at my lentils again.'

On the day following the Harvest Festival the gifts will be sorted and then distributed amongst the old-age pensioners living locally. The juniors love this occasion. They spend half of the morning making cards which say 'With love from the children of St. Claude's School' and then after playtime and again in the afternoon they go out armed with names and addresses and bundles of gifts. But whilst the children enjoy this diversion from lessons I'm not too sure about the feelings of the local old folk. Those getting the packets of tea and tins of biscuits are probably happy enough, but I've a shrewd idea that the recipients of the lychees, avocado pears and tins of bean sprouts reckon they've had a raw deal. Needless to say the gifts are very carefully sorted in the office before distribution and I make sure that tins rusty or 'blown', home-made preserves covered in mould, and toxic-looking jars of foreign unidentifiables are given to Mr Potts for disposal.

By the third week in October we are having trouble with fireworks in Mr Appleby's classroom, and this reminds me to book the ROSPA man to come and give us an illustrated lecture on Bonfire Night Dangers. I am unconvinced of the wisdom of this annual engagement. A different film is brought along each year, but the theme is always the same – telling the story of some children who do silly things with fireworks around a bonfire and end up with burnt fingers and bandaged heads. The moral undoubtedly impresses those good little girls who would, anyway, spend bonfire evening standing beside Mummy and holding sparklers, but the little thugs who enjoy throwing bangers into Mr Appleby's stationery cupboard or amongst Mrs Potts' brooms are, I think, encouraged to prove how much cleverer they are than the twits in the film.

Last year's ROSPA show was particularly unsuccessful.

After the film had ended and when Mr Masterton was thanking our visitor and saying how we had all learnt a lesson from the story, there were sudden screams from the infants who were sitting cross-legged on the floor. Little girls jumped up clutching their skirts around their knees; little boys scrabbled away on all fours. There were two fireworks popping and spluttering amongst them. Some of the junior boys were giggling; others were looking at Mr Masterton with a delighted and expectant 'what's-he-going-to-do-about-this-one' expression on their faces. The ROSPA man, who had been operating his projector from a trestle table at the back of the hall, looked uneasily at the junior boys nudging and punching each other just in front of his table. Smiling nervously ('I-don't-know-how-to-control-them-so-I'll-pretend-it's-all-good-fun') he hastily packed up all his equipment. Mr Scott jumped forward and dealt with the fireworks, and Mr Masterton sent everyone back to their classrooms except the junior boys, who had to stay behind for a lecture and cross-examination. The culprit was not discovered.

(These mass cross-examinations never work – but during the playtimes and dinnertimes that follow them there will always be a sneaky trickle of tell-tale children prepared to come to Mr Masterton's office. Unfortunately there are always so many tell-tales – some of whom are obviously settling old scores – implicating so many different children (all of whom loudly deny their guilt) that we rarely identify the true villain. Another curious fact that I have noticed: when little boys want to tell tales they come alone and try to sneak in unobserved by their friends; when little girls come to tell tales they come in a posse and with loud accusing voices.)

Hallowe'en is usually observed only by Mrs Snow's class who make funny masks and models of black witches upon broomsticks. Poppy Day is the responsibility of the children from Mr Appleby's class who take it in turns to spend ten minutes or so each day during the second week of November in trailing around the classes with a collecting tin and a tray of poppies. But before the middle of November is reached plans are already being made for the most exhausting festival of the school year. Christmas.

The arrangements for Christmas are so complex that it

takes several staff meetings to sort them out. There is the Christmas Bazaar to start with. This will be held during the first week of December. In the last week of term each class must have a party – but the dates must be decided upon quickly because mums have to be organised to help, games have to be planned, cartoon films must be hired and 'disco' equipment borrowed. The infant children will receive a visit from Father Christmas (on a date agreed with Major Darnall) and someone has to buy all the presents for the sack and wrap them up. The school has to be decorated with paper chains, tinsel, stars and reindeers; the internal Christmas postal system has to be set up and Christmas cards and calendars made. But whilst all these events have to be *planned* well in advance, the scurry of activity involved in carrying them out doesn't take up much more than the last week of term. The event which dominates the life of the school from the autumn half-term holiday until the end-of-year break is the Christmas Concert.

Mr Masterton would really like the whole school to co-operate in a single production, with a few children from each class taking part. Everyone else agrees with this in principle – but they can never agree upon what that single production should be. Mrs Snow would like to write a special Christmas play for the school. Mr Appleby agrees that the Christmas production should be something *new* but he favours a large-scale musical production. (Mr Appleby likes large-scale musical productions. One year he wanted us to put on a school version of *Jesus Christ Superstar*, and another occasion he was trying to push the Daniel Jazz. He once even found something called The Bethlehem Be-Bop which he alone thought would be highly suitable.) Miss Krantz doesn't agree with either suggestion and insists that we must put on a Nativity play. 'CHRISTMAS WOULDN'T BE CHRISTMAS WITHOUT A NATIVITY PLAY' she informs us each year. Mr Scott and Mr Singleton say nothing at the Christmas Concert staff meetings. Mr Singleton is silent because we all know he disapproves of any teaching time being wasted on rehearsing for the Christmas Concert, and Mr Scott – who never plans anything – just hopes that the others will finally agree on something that he can join in with. But there is never any agreement and every year the decision is made that each class will put on a little concert of fifteen minutes length, with the infant classes doing their little pieces during an afternoon and the juniors putting on an evening performance.

Within a week of this staff meeting a second one is called so that each teacher can reveal their Christmas plans and come to some agreement about taking it in turns to have use of the hall stage for rehearsals. At this second meeting last year Mrs Snow told us that she had written a little play for her class. It was about a family of children who wanted lots of expensive things from the supermarket for Christmas, but in the end gained great happiness out of making toys for each other from Mother's leftover curtains. (The year before, Mrs Snow's class play was about a family of discontented bunny rabbits who wanted to eat the delicious turnips growing in the next-door field, but in the end settled happily for the carrots growing at home. Every Christmas Mrs Snow has the same theme. I think it is the philosophy expressed by Maeterlinck in *The Blue Bird* . . . and Mrs Snow believes in improving on it annually.) Miss Krantz said that her class was doing a Nativity play because 'CHRISTMAS WOULDN'T BE CHRISTMAS WITHOUT A NATIVITY PLAY'. Mr Appleby, with a nod and wink, said that he and Roger Scott were going to put on a pantomime that was All his Own Idea. Mr Singleton said nothing. We all knew that Mr Singleton's class would sing three carols and give three Christmas readings. The previous year it had been O Come all ye Faithful, Away in a Manger and Good King Wenceslas, and readings from Thackeray, Dickens and W. H. Hudson. The year before that it was Hark the Herald Angels Sing, Silent Night and We Three Kings, with readings from Shakespeare, Sir Philip Sydney and Samuel Pepys. Bearing in mind Mr Singleton's logical and progressive thinking I guessed (rightly) that for last year's concert we would be treated to two joyful and one sad carol accompanied by readings from the Christmas thoughts of three 20th century writers.

During the first week of December it suddenly occurs to everyone that we've only got a fortnight left before the week of festivities is upon us. The staffroom table becomes cluttered with Christmas paper, tinsel, cloth, and boxes of

Things. There is always somebody wanting to wrap presents, getting in the way of someone else who is trying to run up somthing quickly on the sewing machine, and there is always someone on their knees cutting out large pieces of crepe paper over which everyone else has to step. Tempers are short. Miss Krantz is always the first to complain of exhaustion and overwork and the children, sensing that *this* end of term is going to be something special, become cheeky in class – and screaming maniacs in the playground.

I sit and type carols. As well as my frantic routine end-of-term activity with accounts (a particularly exasperating exercise at the end of the Christmas term when everyone is raiding the petty cash tin or the School Fund tin daily – 'I just *have* to buy some more glitter-glow/crackers/aerosol snow-spray/red felt' – and they always forget the receipt) I have to enter into the spirit of the thing and 'be a dear and just type out for me a play/speech/few poems/carols'. The trouble with typing carols is that I can't resist singing them as I go along. Not being a very accurate typist by nature, I find that a musical accompaniment of my own making causes mistakes even more bizarre than usual to manifest themselves. (Mrs Snow – who is familiar enough with my typing to know she can never trust it – was able to save her little ones from having to struggle with Away in a Manager last year, but the juniors, on the other hand, were delighted to bellow out my carol of While Shepherds Watched their Clocks by Night.)

On the day of the parties no-one even *pretends* to do any school work. In each classroom a table will be set aside for the cakes, crisps and biscuits that have been brought in to school by the children. All the morning the staffroom will be cluttered with parents making jellies and Instant Whip trifles and quarrelling about space in the fridge, and the children will be either having final rehearsals for their concerts, or being kept quiet making place-mats and funny hats for the party. The two infant classes always join forces in the Assembly Hall for their celebration (which includes a visit from Father Christmas) but the other classes stay in their rooms.

Mr Singleton, who believes in keeping things firmly under control even at party times, has each child sitting at its desk as usual whilst a responsible bevy of girls act as 'waitresses' to ensure that everyone has a fair share of food. Crackers will be distributed, about ten minutes allowed for a subdued amount of 'larking about', and then Mr Singleton – whose face manages to look grimmer than usual when underneath a crumpled paper hat – will give out paper and pencils for the 'games'. Mr Scott, of course, organises nothing. His room will be a happy shambles of cake, jelly and spilt orange juice for the first hour – and then he will have everyone sitting down to watch television for the rest of the afternoon.

Mr Masterton spends most of the party time hovering about in the hall with the infants. I think this is partly because he wishes to be with Major Darnall as he does his Yo! Ho! Ho! Father Christmas act, but also because he wants to be as far away as possible from Mr Appleby's classroom, where the blackout curtains will be drawn across the windows, the tables and chairs pushed back to the walls, and a record player will be thumping out a noise which will be as distorted as it is deafening. Last year I tried to get in to see Mr Appleby during his party time; he had left his car lights on, and I thought he might like to be told about it. But I couldn't get near him, neither could I make myself heard above the piercing shrieks of the children and the rhythmic thumps and yells from the record player. When my eyes had become accustomed to the gloom I could just make out the heavy figure of Mr Appleby in the corner bending over the trestle table full of food. His back was to the mass of children in the room. Some were leaping up and down, some were writhing about on the floor, and they all seemed to be screaming. I backed out of the room deciding that Mr Appleby's car lights were going to have to stay on . . . and I wondered which of the floor-writhing bodies was Marlene's.

The noise in the Assembly Hall where the infants have their party is more of a happy chirruping sound – like a pre-roosting flock of starlings. The children sit on their little chairs which will be drawn up to tables covered with crepe paper and loaded with party food. Some children giggle excitedly and mess about with handfuls of crisps, whilst others earnestly and steadily push food into their mouths. But there will always be one or two who are bemused by the whole affair and who sit solemnly beneath their paper hats waiting for somebody to tell them what to do. There are usually plenty of mums at the infants' party. Parents Types 1, 2 and 3 stand around in little groups chatting, or wander about vaguely with plates of food. Each parent Type 4 stands stolidly behind its own child's chair and ferries cakes, sandwiches, jellies and trifle to its plate. Parents Type 5 do not come to the parties. Mrs Snow always manages to look very attractive in a cleverly made and flattering paper hat, and Miss Krantz always eats a lot of sausage rolls.

At the end of the afternoon when the last child has left, clutching its paper hat, some tinsel bauble and a present, and crunching its way through the sea of crisps over the corridor floor, Mr and Mrs Potts and Mrs Penfold move in with sweeping brushes, mops and dustpans. This is the one occasion when Mrs Penfold doesn't grumble; she can always take home a large plastic bag of half-eaten buns, ham sandwiches and currant cake for her dog.

The day following the parties is traditionally Concert Day – with last-minute rehearsals going on all morning. Last year Mrs Snow's class performed the little play she had written, and the children from Miss Krantz's class, with earnest piping voices, told us about the birth of Christ. There were a few awkward moments. One of the solemnly marching wise men had his long trailing gown stepped on by his colleague behind, and sat down with a sudden thump, scattering his casket of jewels. The helpful shepherds scuttled about retrieving the rolling plastic beads and pieces of Lego and restored them to the tumbled wise man who looked on the point of tears (but didn't – quite). Joseph's gown was a bit too short and revealed a pair of very dirty plimsolls, and Mary – who was obviously in need of another examination by the School Nurse – couldn't stop scratching her head. But the story was told, with all its startling wonder . . . and only one boorish dad laughed aloud when the leading wise man announced his gift of 'Gold Myrrh and Frankenstein'.

Last year's junior Christmas Concert was memorable because of the extremely large audience it attracted. The hall was packed and smelled strongly of damp clothes and sweat. I think that every junior's mum and dad, brothers and sisters and a few aunties were there. (I seem to remember that there was a strike of television technicians that evening.) Mr Singleton's class came on first. All the children were lined up on the stage; the first row sitting cross-legged, the second row kneeling and the third row standing. They were all very tidily dressed. One boy came forward and recited, by heart, a short piece about a war-time Christmas by H. E. Bates and then all the children stood up and sang the carol Ding Dong Merrily on High. Then a very self-conscious little girl, with her eyes fixed on a point near the ceiling at the back of the hall, quoted from *A Country Christmas* by Alison Uttley. This was followed by a beautifully sung solo of I Sing of a Maiden accompanied by three children on recorders. A final reading of *A Welsh Christmas* by Dylan Thomas (by a boy who rather overdid the indeed-to-goodness accent) was rounded off by a cheerful rendering of Deck the Hall with Boughs of Holly.

There was about fifteen minutes of confusion and scuffling behind the curtains whilst the stage was rearranged for the Appleby/Scott joint performance, and then Jason Spragg, dressed as a jester, and swinging a ball on the end of a string, came in front of the curtain to announce that we were going to watch a performance of St. Claude's Corker Christmas Carve-Up – a Pantomime for Punks and Parents. Jason moved back and the curtain went up. I didn't really get the drift of the fifteen minutes that followed. All the children from both classes seemed to be involved and there was a lot of rushing on and off the stage by various characters.

At one point Father Christmas came on strumming a guitar, and there was a line-up of disco-dancing angels. Marlene Coggins, with half-closed eyes and swaying hips – her nightdress low at the bosom and tight at the waist – led the Heavenly Choir. She was followed and earnestly watched by May Watts, wearing a brushed-nylon white nightdress tied at the waist but too long and held up grimly by May as she tried to imitate Marlene's snake-like movements. But whereas Marlene went slither, slither, wiggle, May went scuffle, scuffle, hop; her skinny flea-bitten calves pumping up and down with determination. Each angel wore a halo of tinsel and white crepe paper. May's was becoming a little looser with each hop, and ended up lodged firmly upon the top of her glasses, making it necessary for her to jut her

178

chin in order to keep her eyes on Marlene's feet yet at the same time retain her halo. The disco-dancing angels pranced and shuffled across the stage, followed by Jason Spragg who, I am sure, was trying to trip up the last one with his swinging ball on a string. The performance finished with the entire cast on stage singing She'll be coming round St. Clau-aude's when she comes, and the audience cheered and stamped their applause.

As the term draws to a close so plans are made for the Staff Christmas Luncheon. Mrs Snow decorates the staffroom table with a tasteful arrangement of crepe paper, serviettes, candles and a floral display, and Mr Masterton adds several bottles of white wine. Mrs Beagle always lays on a splendid feast of turkey, sprouts and roast potatoes, followed by mince pies, custard and a Christmas pudding. The pudding obviously contains nourishment and alcoholic good cheer to such an extent that I really feel she should lay aside a few of these for her National Emergency food cupboard. The day of the staff luncheon is when Mr Masterton gives the ancillary staff their gifts and thanks everyone for their good service over the past year. Last year Mr Masterton gave Mrs Beagle a bottle of supermarket red wine of unknown make and obscure vintage – and was slightly embarrassed when she presented him, in return, with a 2-litre bottle of Harvey's Club Amontillado. (Several people gave Mrs Beagle bottles last year, and I remmber that I had to call a taxi to take her home at 3 p.m. becamse she wasn't feeling very well.)

On the last morning of term the frantic Christmas activity suddenly goes into reverse as tinselled trees are dismantled, wall displays torn down and stuffed into wastepaper baskets, paper chains, stars and angels are removed from ceilings, the St. Claude's Christmas post box is shoved back into the stock cupboard and the children are urged to collect together their cards and calendars ready to take home. Dinner is always a scratch affair of odds and ends that Mrs Beagle wants to clear out from her store cupboard and refrigerator before the holidays, and I try to ensure that any white wine left over from yesterday's staff luncheon is secreted in the stock cupboard as 'secretary's perks'. During the afternoon nobody except me has anything left to do and the entire school gathers in the Assembly Hall for the final event of the term – the carol service. I certainly haven't time to go up to the Hall, but I prop the office door open so that I can hear the carols.

For me the end of every term brings a strange assortment of feelings: bad temper because *I'm* busy and no-one else is; relief that it will soon be over; wistfulness at the passing of another term; glad to be seeing the back of the children, yet looking forward to seeing them next term . . . but the end of the Christmas term is particularly poignant. Perhaps it has something to do with the old meaning of Christmas; perhaps it has something to do with the passing of the winter solstice; or perhaps it has something to do with the half-bottle of white wine at my elbow as I struggle to balance the petty cash account.

The last carol, Mr Singleton's faviourite, comes echoing down the corridor . . .

> In the bleak mid-winter frosty wind made moan
> Earth stood hard as iron, water like a stone . . .

I can imagine them al up in the hall, watching Mr Singleton carefully; even Jason Spragg and his cronies will be standing straight and earnest, concentrating on the carol . . .

> Snow had fallen, snow on snow, snow on snow . . .

I suppose they're not a bad lot of kids really. (This is an *excellent* drop of Soave!) . . . I know that Marlene's mouth will be open in a wide 'O', but May will be looking very serious and mumbling (she always seems to forget the words) — and I bet that one dirty fawn sock is pulled up to her knee and the other is round her ankle . . .

> In the bleak mid-winter, lo-ong ago.

The next verse is the quiet one. Mr Singleton will be spreading his arms and flapping his scrawny hands in a hushing movement – and the children respond . . .

> What can I give him, poor as I am?
> If I were a shepherd I would bring a lamb . . .

They're not King's College – but they're doing their best!

> If I were a wise man I would do my part,
> Yet what I can I give him, give my *heart*

(Marlene's voice soars like pure silver) . . .

> Give my heart.

CHAPTER TWELVE

Outings – and Other Diversions

There is a distinct lack of zest about the start of term in January. Everyone asks 'Did you have a good Christmas?' without wishing to hear the answer; new projects are started half-heartedly; children are coughing and complaining of sore throats, and within a couple of days the heating system will fail. This is the term when Miss Krantz will have one or two days off a fortnight (with her 'chest'), Mr Scott will eagerly comb the vacancy bulletin for a new job, and Mrs Snow will throw a party (and Mr Appleby will be absent the next day with 'tummy trouble'). As the school year permits only three terms, and one of the traditional seasons has therefore to be omitted, there is no such thing as a Winter Term in school terminology. These cold, dark and dreary days at the start of the year are known as 'Spring'.

On 14th February all the infants will make Valentine cards (mostly 'To Mummy' but some 'To Mr Masterton') but the junior children, who sneer at such trivia, are enthusiastic only for netball and football. Our teams are not very successful. Our repeated failures at netball matches are usually explained away because 'the other girls were so much bigger' but such excuses can't be put forward for our football team who have built for themselves a reputation for fouling, abusive language, threatening behaviour and general skulduggery to such an extent that Mr Appleby sometimes has difficulty arranging fixtures. Our football team's lack of skill prevented them from actually winning any matches last winter, but through sheer brute force they achieved a remarkable number of goals (mostly scored by Jason Spragg) as well as three dislocated kneecaps, four split lips, and one case of concussion (also, I suspect, scored by Jason Spragg.) But their enthusiasm for the game is unbounded, and the greatest punishment for any junior boy who has committed some misdemeanour in school is to be banned from football.

On the day that a match is to be played our junior boys will spend the lunchtime doing aggressive things in the playground with each other and a football (an activity which is called 'practising'), and on their return from the match they will tumble out of Mr Appleby's car in a noisy bunch, announcing the result of the game at the tops of their voices to the street in general and the school in particular. The rest of the school will be quietly working in their classrooms, but our returning bunch of heroes are always convinced that we have all been anxiously waiting to hear their news. 'Four goals!' they bellow down the corridor. Muddy, bloody and panting they swing their boots and swagger back to their classroom. 'Four goals! Four goals! . . . Up St. Claude's!' There will always be one dishevelled thug who thrusts open the office door and bellows the result at me – just in case I hadn't heard. The fact that they actually *lost* the game is not considered worth mentioning.

Fortunately, this term is a short one. The half-term holiday falls at the end of February and then, once we are into March, there is a noticeable lifting of spirits in the staffroom. With the coming of spring, plans can be made for projects outside the school . . . and the Easter holiday is not far off. But before the Easter break Mrs Snow's little ones will make models of fluffy yellow chickens, and Miss Krantz's class will make Easter cakes, and all the children in the school will be presented with an Easter egg, paid for out of the School Fund. There is also the St. Claude's Easter Concert.

The Easter Concert at St. Claude's is the main musical event of the year. So far as Mr Singleton is concerned it is also the *most important* event of the year. It is the one occasion about which he is neither cynical nor disparaging. Since the Christmas holiday he will have been working on part of the score of a religious oratorio (usually The Messiah) in order to adapt it for performance by a school orchestra and choir, and the rehearsals start in earnest after half-term. Every lunchtime and on several evenings he will persuade or bully the children to stay in the Assembly Hall for practice, and our musical parents are encouraged to put in as much time as they can spare at school. The performance itself is always polished and inspiring. Mr Singleton retires next Easter and will stage his last concert on the final day of term. After next year Easter will just not be the same – for St. Claude's or for Mr Singleton.

Treats and outings – known today as 'Educational Visits' (the wording is important; we get VAT refunded on all expenses incurred on 'Educational Visits') – are now an accepted part of the curriculum and they take place all year round. But there are a lot more of them during the summer term. One summer Mr Masterton, in a mood of fatherly 'togetherness' suggested that the school shut down for a day and we all went off for a day trip together. The occasion was not a success. We hired two double-decker buses to take us to the seaside and before we had reached the end of the road red-faced infant mums were complaining about the bad language of the juniors and someone let off a stink bomb. When we arrived at the seaside there was a state of milling confusion in the bus park because no-one could agree what to do. The infants wanted to go and play on the sands; the junior boys, without asking permission from anyone, set off in the direction of the Amusement Arcade, and little groups of junior girls demanded to be allowed to 'go round the shops'.

In the event the weather turned nasty and we all came home early – which was just as well. Groups of grizzling infants and shivering bad-tempered mums lurked most of the time in the wind shelters along the front, Jason Spragg 'accidentally' pushed another boy, fully clothed, into the paddling pool, and one of the junior girls was caught shoplifting in Woolworths. Miraculously, no child was actually drowned, damaged, prosecuted or lost . . . and we were all extremely relieved when the double-decker buses unloaded us back at school again. The all-in-together experiment was not tried again and each teacher now decides independently of the rest of the school what the class outings shall be.

Mrs Snow usually manages to fit in two during the summer term. On one occasion – with a fleet of cars driven by helpful parents – she will take her class to the local Zoological Gardens, and the second visit will be a coach trip to a stately home – provided that the grounds of the stately home sport a toddlers' roundabout, swing and slider park. The main requirements for Mrs Snow's outings are plenty of space for the children to run about in and something interesting to go and look at indoors in case it rains. She encourages plenty of mums to come along, and the outings are always a success. In the days that follow, the children will paint pictures of 'What we saw at the Zoo', or 'What we saw at the Old House'.

Miss Krantz, who each summer takes her class to a Wild Life Park, doesn't seem to have such co-operative parents. She complains that those who do volunteer to help will, more often than not, wander around the paths of the park in a gossiping gaggle, whilst the children they are supposed to be supervising run amok in the woods. The Wild Life Park is administered by the Local Authority (via the City Museum's Natural History Unit) and is a highly documented piece of ground. Visiting school parties (who have to book up well in advance) are issued with clipboards holding a sketch map and a large workbook which contains outlines of leaves, trees, birds and mammals which the children are invited to look for. The park itself has well cared-for and signposted paths, with notice boards at every junction telling the visitor what can be seen at this point, as well as 'you are here' maps, in case they are lost. Litter bins, tastefully concealed behind rustic log holders, can be found at every corner and there is a picnic place (more rustic log furniture) which has a corrugated plastic roof in case it rains. The lavatories are in the coach park, which also contains a drinking fountain, and a large bird-identification chart in a glass case. The children usually return from these outings muddy, rosy-cheeked and in high spirits. During the days which follow they will write accounts which tell how, 'We saw a lot of trees and Hannah stepped into some dog dirt on the path' or 'Lots of animals live in the woods. We sat on the grass to eat our sandwiches and Miss Krantz got mud on her skirt.'

Mr Scott loves outings. His main summer outing is usually to the seaside (although one year he took them all to London to visit the Tower) but he also takes his class ice-skating or roller-skating; on trips up the river by barge; to the Zoo, to the Museum and to whatever exhibition is currently being mounted at the Art Gallery. Mr Scott can always produce excellent educational reasons for all these outings and usually manages to charm an army of mums to come along and help. But even with no mums available Mr Scott will often make a sudden decision on a bright sunny day to take his class out on The Hill 'to practise map reading', or for a walk through the old docks area 'to study architecture'.

Mr Singleton takes his class for four outings each year. Once a term they will spend a morning out on The Hill to check on the seasonal tree, plant and animal life; and once a year they will visit the Natural History Department of the City Museum. None of his visits involves spending any money, neither does he call upon parents to help. But on the occasion of his walk to the Museum he likes me to go along too. He marches at the head of the crocodile of children, whilst I bring up the rear. On his visits to The Hill Mr Singleton always avoids the tidy part where The Authority has laid down formal flower beds and a water garden, and takes his class instead to the scrubby area filled with blackberry bushes, rank grass and gnarled hawthorn trees. In winter the children are asked to note the shape of the bare trees and the remains of nests hanging in the tangle of old bushes; their attention is drawn to the songs of thrush and robin and they are told to keep their eyes skinned for the blue and great tits. In springtime the children will see the opening of the celandines, coltsfoot, ground ivy and speedwell. They will see the strong thrust of the new elder shoots and the voluptuous unfolding of the chestnut buds – and they will be asked to listen carefully for the first willow warbler. In summer the wild patch on The Hill will be a riot of cow parsley, valerian, ragwort and buddleia, where tortoiseshells, red admirals, peacocks, painted ladies, commas and other butterflies dance all day.

When the children march back to school after an outing

to The Hill they don't sit and write accounts or draw pictures; they keep lists. Mr Singleton runs a Spotters' Club and encourages the children to keep lists of plants, birds or butterflies that they have personally identified upon The Hill. Some children are very competitive, and there will always be one or two enthusiasts who will insist that they saw a bee-eater or hoopoe or a swallowtail butterfly. But many of the children are bored and feel cheated that they can't go ice-skating like Mr Scott's lot.

Every year there is an 'Educational Camp' organised by Mr Appleby. Most of the children from the top class and some of the older ones from Mr Singleton's class will go off by coach on a Monday morning, and we won't see them again until late afternoon on the Friday. The office, during that first half-hour on the morning of departure, is a chaotic jumble of bulging haversacks, suitcases tied with string, plastic carrier bags, and tearful mums giving last-minute warnings and exhortations. There will be children urgently wanting to telephone home for something forgotten; there will be Mr Appleby ruthlessly confiscating radio sets and sheath knives . . . and there will always be someone who has something nasty leaking from the bottom of a rucksack. It is my responsibility to remember the sick bucket and the First Aid kit – which are the last items to be loaded on the coach.

To take about forty young children away for a week's camp under canvas is an awesome responsibility. Another member of the St. Claude's staff will always accompany Mr Appleby and his party of children and we always call on the help of a student or two from the local polytechnic. There is a shuffling around of children in the remaining classes at school and we are allowed to take on a supply teacher for the week. My involvement (principally to do with the collecting of money in the preceding weeks) ends with the handing over of the sick bucket, and when the loaded coach eventually pulls away a blessed peace, echoing and dusty, falls over the school. In the days that follow we keep remarking to each other how quiet it is. The infants play prettily in the playground, which now seems vast and empty, and it is possible to walk freely along the school corridors without the danger of a child hurtling into one's midriff at every corner.

As well as the week at camp, Mr Appleby likes to ensure that his class has at least one day's outing during the summer term. Being well aware of the risks involved in taking a mixed party of juniors to stately homes or museums, he usually ends up at The Authority's Wild Life Park where, even armed with clipboards, the children cannot do much immediately visible damage. Generally speaking Mr Appleby is more interested in the character-forming benefits of a day in the woods (like staying out all day even though it is pouring with rain) rather than the noting of the flora and fauna . . . which is just as well, remembering the disastrous consequences when Mr Appleby decided, on one autumn trip, to take an interest in fungi. With his book in his hand he had no difficulty in pointing out Chanterelle and Shaggy Ink Cap, but then got carried away with confidence and in order to prove the edibility of something he identified as 'Wood Mushroom' he ate three or four choice specimens.

In view of what subsequently happened I think Mr Appleby had confused *Agaricus silvicola* (edible and good) with *Rhodophyllus sinuatus* (poisonous) because some twenty minutes later (according to some of the mums accompanying the party) Mr Appleby turned white, then a shade of deathly green – and suddenly crumpled up on the path where he was violently and prolongedly sick. A trembling and perspiring Mr Appleby, supported by two mums, was then taken back to the coach and the day's outing was cut short. As a demonstration of the hazards of eating wild fungi, Mr Appleby could not have thought up a more effective lesson. However, the children – shocked and horrified at the time – remembered the occasion with glee, and without exception each child's subsequent drawing of the day's outing included a cartoon picture of Mr Appleby being sick in the bushes.

The main all-school event of June is the Summer Fayre (already described in Chapter 10) and before we break up for the long summer holiday there is the last of the summer festivals – Sports Day.

By regular arrangement with the Municipal Authority we are allowed each year to hold our Sports Day on The Hill. Having to hop, skip, jump, run or stagger on three legs across the angle of a one in ten slope adds an interesting dimension to the competition and, by common agreement, no events are organised which involve balls or anything else liable to go hurtling down the hill.

The infants are, as usual, charming. I can remember one year when Mrs Snow had a line-up of a dozen little ones who, it turned out, didn't know what Sports Day was all about. 'Ready, Steady, GO!' said Mrs Snow . . . Go? . . . Go where? A clutch of them turned and raced down the hill towards school; two ran crying to where their mothers were sitting; one little girl stood stock still staring at Mrs Snow and waiting for further explanation, and one little boy who quickly got the idea started running across the field to where Miss Krantz was waving her arms about.

The juniors race with determination and belligerence. The team events inspire raucous cheers, encouraging yells and recriminating jeers. Mr Appleby organises the events, with much shouting and waving of his race chart; Mr Singleton usually keeps the score and Mrs Snow sees to the orange squash. Miss Krantz and I look after all the equipment and Mr Scott wades in to sort out the fights. It is an exhausting occasion for everybody. The children love Sports Day; the parents enjoy coming to watch . . . but if it happens to pour with rain and the event is called off, the staff hide their disappointment remarkably well.

The Sports Day of one year is much like the Sports Day of another year, but there is one incident which stands out in my memory . . . the year that Sebastian's mother came to watch. It was a very hot afternoon. There was an oppressive feeling of thunder in the air and when the sky over the city turned blue-black and the first rumbles were heard we knew we might suddenly have to abandon sports and take shelter back at school. Sebastian's mother had arrived early to watch the sports. She was with her boyfriend – and she was drunk. The couple settled down upon the grass a little distance away from other parents and Sebastian's mum – after a vague bleary look at the first couple of races – lay back and appeared to be sleeping.

We had got as far as the junior sack race when it became obvious that Sebastian's mother's boyfriend was taking more interest in her than in the race. He pushed a few strands of hair away from her face and kissed her nose one or two times. His hand, hovering gently around her chin and throat, then moved down to fumble with the buttons of her blouse, and the lady stirred slightly – turning her face towards him. Miss Krantz, with flushed cheeks, stamped past the couple clapping hands and roaring 'NOW DON'T LEAVE YOUR SACKS ON THE FIELD CHILDREN: BRING THEM TO ME' and Sebastian's mother's boyfriend stopped fumbling and propped himself up on one elbow. But Sebastian's mother was now having interesting ideas, and one drowsy hand reached out to her boyfriend and tugged gently at his shirt. During the running of the junior team relay they exchanged long and loving kisses.

Several other parents nearby darted indignant glances at the couple and then looked expectantly across the field to where Mr Masterton was earnestly studying the score sheet. 'It's a pity we don't have a bucket of water,' Mrs Snow hissed at me. And the gods must have heard her. Just as the boyfriend started groping beneath Sebastian's mother's dirndl skirt there was a terrific clap of thunder, and the heavens opened. 'Back to school!' commanded Mr Masterton instantly (the quickest decision I have ever known him make), and we all hurried down the hill. All, that is, except Sebastian's mother and her boyfriend, who stayed stuck to the hillside going about their own earnest business undeterred by the hailstones bouncing upon them.

By the last week of term all the final arrangements will have been made for the children who are transferring to secondary education, and most of the children will have spent some time visiting their new school. Now that parents have (theoretically) a little more say in the choice of secondary school these arrangements have to be started quite early in the year – when all parents involved will be sent details of the local comprehensive school and an application form upon which to indicate their acceptance or rejection of the place available for their child.

The parents deal with these forms in a predictable way. Most children of Type 1 parents will bring back their forms by return – neatly endorsed with the comment that arrangements have already been made for the child to go to a private school. Some of Type 3 parents accept places at the local comprehensive school, others choose the local private school which follows the Rudolph Steiner system of education. Parents Type 4, after a lot of heart-searching and delay, endorse their form agreeing to the arrangements made. Parents Type 5 lose the form – but the children always turn up at the local comprehensive school on the first day of the new term. Parents Type 2 sometimes surprise us. Having frequently and articulately defended the comprehensive system of education some of them, at this moment of truth, now have doubts. 'Of course I totally support the comprehensive system *in principle* but I don't think it's *quite right for Gideon*.' And Gideon will sit an entrance exam for the local grammar school.

Nothing is planned for the last few days of term. The pace of activity has slackened almost to a full stop. In the classroom lessons become less important than 'clearing up'. Miss Krantz and Mrs Snow both claim to be exhausted, but now that the end is in sight it is more of a statement than a complaint. On the last day of term all equipment has to be locked away (because of the Holiday School) and all notices and drawings must be removed from walls (because of Mr Potts' annual clean-up). Everyone goes about these tasks in a relaxed happy manner. No-one, except me, is pressed for time.

Morning Assembly on the last day of term is made a special occasion and Mr Masterton always gives a thoughtful talk along the line of now-that-we-are-setting-out-on-life's-pathway for the benefit of the children who will be leaving us. But it always seems to me that remarkably few children consider the transition from primary to secondary education to be of any special significance. Mostly they set-out-on-life's-pathway looking cheerfully ahead and without a backward glance at the school which has been a second home to them since, perhaps, they were five years old. Moreover, I have noticed that when the children have been at secondary school for a term or two they become different people – and their reactions when they see me in the street differ accordingly. Some come rushing up and greet me like an old friend – anxious to show me their new uniform or to talk about their achievements. Others seem to be troubled by embarrassment and they sneak past with averted eyes and say nothing.

But although on their last day at primary school most children rush out of school in their usual manner, some of them at least feel *something*. Last year, when I had finally balanced all my accounts, locked the safe, filed the last documents, filled in all the end of term forms for The Authority and was ready to leave; I went to look for Mr Potts to say goodbye. I knew that he and Mrs Potts would be cleaning somewhere in the school and I looked first in Mr Scott's room. Cushions and crayons were all over the floor, and the posters – torn from the wall but leaving the Sellotape behind – were stuffed into the wastepaper basket. All was orderly in Mr Singleton's room. The desks were lined up; the chairs were placed upon them and there were three faded marks on the wall where 'What to look for in Summer' had been taken down, and where 'What to look for in Autumn' would be placed next term. In Mr Appleby's room tables and chairs lay at all angles and I noticed that a window was broken. There is something disturbingly desolate about a room which has only just emptied itself of a crowd of noisy, boisterous children. Like the acute silence which fills the moment following a thunderous end to a symphony concert, so the emptiness of those rooms was a charged and positive emptiness – an emptiness thick with atmosphere.

Miss Krantz's room was not empty. She was still there, muddling about in one of her cupboards. She didn't seem in a hurry to go home. Mrs Snow's room was neat, with tiny tables and chairs lined up against the wall and the carpet in the Book Corner rolled up. There was no sign of Mr Potts and I turned to go, but a slight movement in the Home Corner caught my eye. Curled up in Mrs Snow's cosy chair, where children sick or sad are comforted, was Marlene Coggins. With Mrs Snow's giant cuddly Snoopy clasped to her bosom Marlene was staring into space. And the tears were rolling down her cheeks.

The End

A SELECTED LIST OF AUTOBIOGRAPHIES AND BIOGRAPHIES AVAILABLE FROM CORGI BOOKS

WHILE EVERY EFFORT IS MADE TO KEEP PRICES LOW, IT IS SOMETIMES NECESSARY TO INCREASE PRICES AT SHORT NOTICE. CORGI BOOKS RESERVE THE RIGHT TO SHOW NEW RETAIL PRICES ON COVERS WHICH MAY DIFFER FROM THOSE PREVIOUSLY ADVERTISED IN THE TEXT OR ELSEWHERE.

THE PRICES SHOWN BELOW WERE CORRECT AT THE TIME OF GOING TO PRESS (DECEMBER '84).

☐	09332 7	GO ASK ALICE	*Anonymous*	£1.50
☐	99065 5	THE PAST IS MYSELF	*Christabel Bielenberg*	£2.50
☐	12553 9	SWINGS AND ROUNDABOUTS	*Angela Douglas*	£2.50
☐	11256 9	DOWN THE VILLAGE STREET	*Peter Douglas*	95p
☐	12242 4	KEEP HIM, MY COUNTRY	*Mary Durack*	£1.95
☐	12095 2	A LIFE IN OUR TIMES	*John K. Galbraith*	£3.95
☐	99066 3	NAMESAKE	*Michel Goldberg*	£1.95
☐	99098 1	AUTUMN OF FURY	*Mohamed Heikal*	£2.95
☐	12191 6	LITTLE RESISTANCE	*Antonia Hunt*	£1.50
☐	12250 5	SIDNEY REILLY: THE TRUE STORY	*Michael Kettle*	£1.75
☐	12033 2	DIARY OF A MEDICAL NOBODY	*Kenneth Lane*	£1.75
☐	23662 8	DON'T FALL OFF THE MOUNTAIN	*Shirley MacLaine*	£1.50
☐	12452 4	OUT ON A LIMB	*Shirley MacLaine*	£2.50
☐	12378 1	CORONER TO THE STARS	*Thomas Noguchi*	£1.95
☐	99051 5	THE ROAD GOES ON FOREVER	*Philip Norman*	£2.50
☐	11961 X	SHOUT!	*Philip Norman*	£2.50
☐	12399 4	ANY FOOL CAN BE A PIG FARMER	*James Robertson*	£1.75
☐	12072 3	KITCHEN IN THE HILLS	*Elizabeth West*	£1.50
☐	11707 2	GARDEN IN THE HILLS	*Elizabeth West*	£1.25
☐	10907 X	HOVEL IN THE HILLS	*Elizabeth West*	£1.50
☐	99097 3	CATCH A FIRE	*Timothy White*	£3.95

All these books are available at your book shop or newsagent, or can be ordered direct from the publisher. Just tick the titles you want and fill in the form below.

CORGI BOOKS, Cash Sales Department, P.O. Box 11, Falmouth, Cornwall.

Please send cheque or postal order, no currency.

Please allow cost of book(s) plus the following for postage and packing:

U.K. Customers—Allow 55p for the first book, 22p for the second book and 14p for each additional book ordered, to a maximum charge of £1.75.

B.F.P.O. and Eire—Allow 55p for the first book, 22p for the second book plus 14p per copy for the next seven books, thereafter 8p per book.

Overseas Customers—Allow £1.00 for the first book and 25p per copy for each additional book.

NAME (Block Letters) . . . .

ADDRESS . . . .

. . . .